JAMES WHALE has enjoyed a successful broadcasting career for over thirty years. The winner of three prestigious Sony Radio Awards (not that he gives a damn), until recently he presented the late-night show on talkSPORT. In 2006, he set up the James Whale Fund for Kidney Cancer, to fund research and raise awareness of the disease (www.jameswhalefund.org). He has previously published *Bald on Top*.

ALMOST
A CELEBRITY

JAMES WHALE

A LIFETIME OF NIGHT-TIME

James Whale

with Shaun Hutson

Michael O'Mara Books Limited

First published in Great Britain in 2007 by
Michael O'Mara Books Ltd
9 Lion Yard, Tremadoc Road
London SW4 7NQ

Revised and updated paperback edition
first published in 2008

Papers used by Michael O'Mara Books Limited are natural, recyclable
products made from wood grown in sustainable forests. The
manufacturing processes conform to the environmental regulations of
the country of origin.

ISBN 978-1-84317-324-3

1 3 5 7 9 10 8 6 4 2

www.mombooks.com

Designed and typeset by e-type

Plate section designed by www.envydesign.co.uk

Printed and bound in Great Britain by CPI Cox & Wyman, Reading, Berks

contents

In the words of my mate Jim Diamond,
I should have known better.

author's acknowledgements

There are many people who will feel that they should have been in this book, and there are those whom I'm sure would have preferred to have been left out – but hey, that's showbiz.

As you'll soon find out from reading this book, there are loads of things that have happened to me along the way. There are also many episodes that I've had to leave out – you can only put so much into one book. Who knows? There may well be another.

There are lots of people I need to thank. Firstly, many thanks to Shaun Hutson and his wife Belinda for making the book happen; to Jeff Chegwin, for getting me off my arse and doing stuff; to Brie Burkeman, my literary agent; to Chris Moyles, for providing the Foreword; and to everyone at Michael O'Mara Books.

My gratitude goes to my family: my son James, for being a quiet, thoughtful person when the rest of us are mad; my son Peter, his wife Adele and all our grandchildren; Melinda's mum Barbara, brother Max and the rest of her family; and my brother Keith, his wife Ruth, and all their family.

Thanks also to my friend Stuart Hobday, his wife Helen and their family, who've lived the life with us since the early nineties; to Janice and Peter Perry, who were there at the very start in the late sixties, and with whom we still enjoy a good night out; to June, my godmother, and her family; and to my cousins Prue and Tessa and the family in Porthcawl. A shout out to Mike Woodcock, for being there; to Peter Straker, for being a mate and bringing high culture into our lives; and to Lisa Voice, for being one of the most extravagant people I have ever met.

Thank you to Luke Goss, his wife Shirley and manager David Wood, with whom we've shared some great adventures over the past couple of years. I hope Luke's life in Hollywood is going to be everything he wants it to be, and I hope it's not going to be too long before we all do something completely mad again.

I must express appreciation to Jim Diamond and his wife Chris, for providing our musical backdrop; to Henry and Martha Cobbold and family for the good times at Knebworth; to Carol Vorderman, her mum Jean and all the Vorder-people; to Eamonn Holmes and his wife Ruth – it's good to have Eamonn back in my life; to Uri Geller, his wife Hannah and brother-in-law Shipi; to Jeff Samuels, for always seeing the funny side; to Graham D, just for being Graham D; to Mike Mansfield and Hillary and all who helped the show at MMTV; to Jonathan Adams, for his advice, friendship and help to Melinda when she needed it most; to Peter Stringfellow, a good mate; and to Max Clifford and his daughter Louise, for being in the picture.

And then there were the jobs: in the seventies, at Metro Radio in Newcastle, Auntie Doreen, Len Groat, Giles Squire, Paddy McD, all the girls who answered the phones, and to the memory of our late boss, Neil Robinson. To those I met at BBC Radio Derby, in particular Terry Christian (who can be a mouthy little sod, but then so can I). In the eighties, at Radio Aire in Leeds – to Geoff Sagerson, for getting me back to night-time radio where I belong; to Carl Kingston; Paul Stead; Ray Stroud; and many, many others at Radio Aire, including Cathryn Sinclair, who added glamour to the wireless. And to the memory of Peter Tate, who did breakfast and was just a nice guy.

In television, there are many people I'd like to thank – in particular Ian Bolt, who originally had the vision of putting my radio show on TV, and Denise Robertson, for being there. Also to the gang: Graham Pollard, Mike Pearson, Gordon Hobbs, Chantelle Rutherford-Brown, and all the others who understood what we were doing.

At Talk Radio, and then talkSPORT, thanks to the first guys who did my show, Peter and Paula; to my old LBC producer who came with me to Talk, Bavin Cook; to The Dominatrix, our Aussie producer, Susan Woodward; to our current producer, Laura; to John Simons (Simo) for being one of the good guys; to Jason Bryant for giving me the job at Talk; and, of course, to my right-hand man, who has been with me longer than anyone else has managed it, Ash. What can I say about this guy? I think I'd better just keep quiet, but thanks, mate, you are appreciated, even if I do shout and throw things at you a lot. To Ian Collins, who's been there longer than I have; and to Alan Brazil and Mike Parry, both natural radio talents. This book is also dedicated to the memory of Mike Dickin – a radio legend – and to his family. A particular mention must go to Bill Ridley, who's guided things with a steady hand, and who was very kind to me while I was ill. I may not show much gratitude, but I feel it.

To those who helped get the James Whale Fund for Kidney Cancer off the ground and to those who have helped in the short time we've been going: so, many thanks to Nick Turkentine, for making it happen; to Nick's wife, Sandy; to Myleene Klass; to my friend Enan Ali at La Raj on the Epsom Downs; to Dave the Decorator and Danny the Landlord for their sterling work; and to Jason Cundey and his lovely wife Lizzie, who've been amazing at getting us publicity.

To David 'the Kid' Jensen; to Steve Wright; to Johnnie Walker, for being an inspiration to me when I was a kid; to Tony Blackburn, for being the ultimate DJ; and to the memory of Tony Windsor, a DJ who had a voice and a presence on radio that inspired many of us.

Last, but by no means least, to Tim O'Brien, my surgeon, without whom you would never have known any of what's to follow.

There are many more people whom I know I'll realize I should have mentioned after this book has gone to print – but, as they say, hey, that's showbiz.

Finally – to Melinda, who sometimes doesn't realize how much I love her.

James Whale, 2007

PICTURE ACKNOWLEDGEMENTS

All pictures courtesy of James Whale's private collection and reproduced with his permission, excepting page 3: Mirrorpix (top and middle), and page 8: CambridgeJones.com (middle).

When I was growing up in Leeds in the late eighties, James Whale's night-time show on Radio Aire was an essential listen. I remember it so clearly. The first hour was 'Do-it-yourself dedications', where listeners would call up, say 'hello' to their friends and then introduce a record. I managed to get on a few times, too.

At eleven o'clock, James told me over the airwaves that I wasn't allowed to listen after the news because I was too young. Unbelievably, I did as the Whale told me and switched off. That was the power that Whale had over his audience.

Occasionally, I would keep listening, thinking that I was doing something naughty.

James's style was absolutely unique. There was nobody like him, and any attempt to copy him seemed weak and poor in comparison. To me, he was a superstar, a true radio legend.

Once, James spent a week telling us that he might introduce Madonna on stage when she played at a local venue the next weekend. As I stood in the crowd at the gig, awaiting the show, James Whale walked on to the stage.

'Told you I'd be here,' he said.

Had Madonna invited him to introduce her? It wouldn't have surprised me.

My dad didn't like him. When I used to speak to Dad about the show, he would always tell me that Whale was rubbish.

'He's garbage, that James Whale. I was listening the other night when he was slagging off some caller. The night before he did exactly the same thing. And last week he was moaning about something else.'

For a man who thought Whale was garbage, Dad seemed to listen to an awful lot of his shows. That is power, and James Whale had it.

For a school project, I once visited the radio studios to take some photos of James. He was polite and charming. By the time we left, my mother thought that he was 'lovely'. The nasty man on the radio was actually a big softie.

James Whale was, and is, an excellent broadcaster. His confident style and fantastic voice make him compelling to listen to.

And by the way, for the record, I never made his fucking tea!

Chris Moyles, 2007

JUST A WORD BEFORE WE BEGIN ...

INTRODUCTION

A recent survey revealed that the most popular song played at funerals is 'My Way', sung by Frank Sinatra. Quite right, too. It's a wonderful song and I'm sure that many people, when it comes to picking a song to play over their send-off, decide that it's appropriate because they feel that they have lived their lives 'their way'.

This book was written my way.

Some people may not agree with the views that are expressed within it – and that's a good thing, because if we all thought the same way, then it would be a pretty dull and boring world.

If you don't like what you're reading, if you're offended by strong views and even stronger language, then I suggest you go and purchase the autobiography of David Blunkett or some *Big Brother* contestant instead. Someone who hasn't really got very much to say to begin with. Someone who doesn't display much passion in their language or life.

With my TV and radio shows, you could reach for the on/off switch if you disliked what I was saying. This book should be easier. If you don't like what I'm saying, then simply throw the book away, or give it to a friend. At the moment, it's still a country of free choice and free will.

For how much longer, I have no idea.

Please feel free to proceed.

I was born Michael Whale, the product of a very rare thing: a loving family. That kind of family unit has always been in fairly short supply and, as the years have passed, it's become even rarer.

On 13 May 1951, I was born into a very ordinary middle-class family in the front room of number four Portway, in Ewell Village, near Epsom Downs, about twenty-five miles south of London. Ewell was a beautiful little village; a small, rural community that supported its own inhabitants with jobs. Not many people commuted to London to work. They seemed quite happy to stay within Ewell itself to earn their living – but then again, these were more sedate times. Times less driven by greed and a desire to earn more money than anyone else you knew.

Ewell today is little more than a suburb of London, but, as I've said, in the 1950s it was a pretty little village in its own right. It had its own butcher, baker and greengrocer, plus a couple of pubs, banks and sweetshops. It was built up around a spring. I believe that during Roman times the area in which I was born was a port, because the river was then so big.

There you go: you weren't expecting a history lesson too, were you? How's that for value for money?

My mum and dad were great. They created a stable, happy environment for me and my younger brother, Keith, to grow up in. My dad, David, worked in the family firm, S&R Whale, which always reminded me of the sixties TV series *The Rag Trade*. The business, which had been set up between the wars, made dresses, aprons and overalls at a little factory on Railton Road in Brixton – a road that became known as 'the front line'. It was made famous by Eddy Grant and several other singers. My father worked there for the first sixteen years of my life, delivering clothes that had been made in the factory. Not high fashion, but the kind of stuff you could buy in the shops in and around south London at that time.

In actual fact, my dad always wanted to be a farmer. He even went to agricultural school in Guildford, Surrey, but his own ambition was never realized. Considering he was brought up in Streatham, London, I suppose it was a rather strange career choice, but sadly for him it was ultimately shelved. The best thing about my dad attending agricultural college was that he met my mum's brother, Norman Price, and consequently my mum. That was how my parents met, through my mum's brother.

My mum, Anne, came from a completely different background to my dad. She was Welsh by birth and a ballet dancer. Two more different people you couldn't imagine. My mum lived in a block of flats in a place called Thames Ditton. One day, my dad decided he'd impress her by taking her for a ride on his motorbike. He rode as fast as he could over a huge pile of coal that had been left outside the flats where my mum lived. He must have thought he was Steve McQueen in *The Great Escape*. My mum wasn't impressed by his antics, though. The experience frightened her to death and it was the last time my dad was ever allowed on his beloved motorbike, and the last time my mum ever went near one. Despite all their differences – in fact, probably because of their differences – they married and, four years later, I came along.

I was brought up in a little two-bedroom semi-detached house in Ewell Village. In the attached part of the semi, next door, lived my grandmother and grandfather on my dad's side, Daphne and Vivien. My grandmother was the archetypal 1920s 'flapper girl', while my grandfather was the sort of dapper guy who'd drive around in an open-top sports car. They didn't have an awful lot of money, but they did have style.

I had a happy early life, I'm sorry to have to tell you. I realize that this kind of book should really be filled with how tough the subject's upbringing was and how terribly they suffered as a child and teenager, but I seem to be an exception. Compared to most kids in the sixties and, more especially, these days, I lived a somewhat unusual and pretty charmed life, living next door to Grandma and Granddad, with no real hardship (not too much money, but certainly enough to be comfortable with).

Our holidays were spent with my mum's parents in Porthcawl in south Wales. Every year, without fail, we went there and played on the beaches. I played around the woods, too. At that stage in my life I wanted either to be a cowboy (I was a big fan of John Wayne) or a knight in armour. In fact, I always used to think I'd been born in the wrong era. I think I'd have been better suited to an age that had more respect and nobility. A time when people cared more for the well-being of others; when they went about their business without causing pain and distress to others.

I wasn't particularly good at school. In fact, I loathed, detested and hated it. One thing that set me apart from many of my fellow students was that I never heard my parents argue (I told you I was the product of a very rare thing). Another was that I wasn't skilled at sport: something pretty much guaranteed to make you unpopular among your peers. I couldn't kick a ball. I couldn't run. This was something of a drawback because all we did was football and cross-country running.

There was one exception. When I was at junior school, about nine years old, we played cricket in the school playground one day. I was one of the fielders. I can remember this as clearly as if it was yesterday. The lad who was wicketkeeping got hit in the face accidentally by the guy who was batting and, to everyone's horror, he died instantly. I remember him lying on the playground, covered by an old brown raincoat that belonged to one of the teachers. It looked like something he might have been given when he was demobbed from his national service. From underneath that tatty old coat, I could see blood seeping.

I remember asking a teacher if the boy was okay, only to be told: 'He's just sleeping.'

'Why have they covered him up?' I wanted to know.

'To keep him warm,' the teacher insisted.

I never really wanted to play cricket again after that.

One of the few positive things ever said about me

when I was at school was how well spoken I was. When I was seven or eight, I had a report from a certain Miss Gentry, who wrote: 'Michael tries very hard, but doesn't seem to understand the basics of reading and arithmetic – but I do think his speaking voice will hold him in good stead for the future.'

My elocution wasn't really a surprise because my mother had always spoken very well, as had the rest of my family, but, at school, I stood out because of my voice. Consequently, I always found myself attempting to fit in by perfecting a more acceptable dumbed-down accent, so I wouldn't be thought a snob. My schizophrenic existence was then compounded by having to return to my usual, and more correct, mode of speech when I returned home every evening. Luckily, I found this sort of double life quite amusing.

It seems unfortunate that a person should be viewed as a snob or 'stuck up' just because they don't speak like Eliza Doolittle before her transformation – but then again, that's just the way of the world. My experience was a precursor to the situation today, when it seems preferable to have the accent of a yob than to enunciate correctly. So many so-called celebrities now attempt to emphasize their humble roots, either by lying about what a terribly hard upbringing they had as kids or by resorting to the simple expedient of speaking like some trainee barrow boy. The 'mockney' has put in an appearance over the past few years: celebrities who do interviews talking like refugees from the East End, when in fact they have enjoyed private-school educations and come from what might be viewed as privileged backgrounds. Why can't these people simply speak the way they were taught to speak? Are they so desperate to be accepted as 'normal' people that they have to put on this act? I find it all a little pathetic.

Despite my attempts to blend in at school by bastardizing my accent, I still used to get regularly beaten up until I had perfected a more moronic tone. Fortunately, this torment by cretins ended when I reached secondary school. Most of the posh kids had gone to the local grammar school, and I found that dropping a few aitches here and there at the secondary modern I attended was sufficient to preserve my well-being. I also became quite tall – though when the senior louts rounded up the first years at break time, my height didn't seem to make much difference. These older yobs used to delight in using us younger kids as horses, riding us in imaginary games. Sometimes it got really quite nasty. Considering Ewell was a quiet and lovely little village, there were some right morons around – most of whom lived on a particularly rough estate just outside Epsom, but unfortunately attended my school.

I suppose the fact that they chose to ride us around like horses at least showed they acknowledged their roots, being from Epsom. Being a stable lad in Epsom was the kind of job the brainless usually gravitated towards, so perhaps they were just getting in some practice for the sort of life that awaited them (although that type didn't usually last or make the grade to become fully-fledged jockeys). I eventually ended my treatment at their hands by the simple expedient of tipping one of them through a plate-glass window one break-time. I was never bothered again after that.

My new hobby also came in handy as far as bullies were concerned. Around the age of eleven, at a village fête, I was lucky enough to see the Nonsuch Bowmen, the local archery club, giving a demonstration of their skills. I immediately thought: 'That is what I want to do.' I could be John Wayne, Robin Hood and Ivanhoe all rolled into one.

My path in life suddenly appeared before me. I got my dad to take me along to some beginners' evenings in Nonsuch Park. From the age of eleven until I left school, I spent every available moment at the archery club, going to tournaments and honing my newly acquired skills and passion. Academic achievement at school became irrelevant to me, just as everything else did when I had a bow in my hand. I was able to concentrate purely on archery. I was in a world of my own when I was practising or competing, and I loved every minute of it.

My newfound interest undoubtedly gave me a certain amount of kudos with my fellow schoolmates, as I've said. Perhaps they feared they'd be shot full of arrows if they bothered me from that point on. My inability to play football, run or participate in other school sports now seemed inconsequential. I was the king of my chosen pastime.

In fact, from the age of fourteen to sixteen, I was convinced I would make my living coaching archery. I was sure it would become a major sport (I was right: it returned as an Olympic sport in 1972). My dreams of becoming the next Robin Hood looked fairly rosy, especially when I was named Surrey's under-sixteen junior champion in 1965.

Looking back on it, that was probably the first time I became aware of how far dedication to and passion for a particular interest could take me. It was a lesson that was to stay with me for the rest of my life and career.

TIME FOR A QUICK BREAK ...

CURSES OF OUR TIMES

Political correctness is, in my opinion, one of the curses of our times. When I sit now and look at the problems people have caused for themselves because of it, I despair. For example, I see people tying themselves in knots trying to avoid using words like 'chairman' and 'manhole', just in case doing so offends any women in the vicinity. We shy away from phrases that might embarrass people of a certain size or skin colour. I never thought that asking for a large black coffee could cause such a palaver. Everyone's so concerned about not causing offence to anyone else, we've forgotten the most important thing about sharing our humanity: actually communicating with one another.

We're following the Americans into the kind of society in which everyone is looking to sue someone else for a perceived wrong. On television, there are adverts encouraging people to take action against their employers if they hurt themselves at work. If we cut our fingers on a paperclip, we're told, we should sue our bosses for being negligent. What bollocks.

Much to my sorrow, the comedian Bernard Manning died recently (June 2007). Bernard was a great funny man and a wonderful human being, and he suffered constantly from the media's obsession with political correctness. The butt of so many 'alternative' comedians' cheap jibes, Bernard appeared many times on my shows both on TV and radio and was always great value. One of the things I take great joy in is the knowledge that Bernard made millions of people happy with his humour and, even better, he made more money than these sanctimonious, 'right-on' wankers will ever make. Can you see Arthur Smith selling 10 million DVDs? No, neither can I. So many of these trendy comics think they occupy the moral high ground because they don't tell jokes that offend people. They also don't tell jokes that amuse people.

Bernard Manning was a guest on my TV show once with Glenys Kinnock and I was winding Glenys up. Bernard jumped to her defence, saying, 'You can't talk to the wife of a future prime minister like that, James.'

'Thank you very much, Mr Manning,' Glenys replied.

I always found that wonderfully ironic – that a politician's wife was being saved by one of the most politically incorrect men ever to walk the planet.

Trevor McDonald, the newsreader (and not the sharpest tool in the box), recently labelled Bernard a 'fat white bastard'. As Bernard himself may have retorted: 'No, a fat, white, *rich* bastard.'

Bernard will be missed by anyone who respects people who speak their minds. Perhaps jealousy was a factor for those who condemned him – because another thing I find both baffling and annoying is the desire for anyone successful to be knocked down.

Unfortunately, this seems to be a peculiarly British trait.

Excellence should be encouraged. Intelligence should be lauded and praised. Those who are genuinely talented, like Bernard, should be held up as examples and role models – those people should be, rather than the one-hit wonders in the pop business or the so-called celebrities who emerge from reality-TV shows. I really find it quite appalling that so many talentless people infest our televisions, newspapers, magazines and airwaves and that society seems to celebrate their lack of ability.

The fact that the money earned by some of these pseudo-celebrities would easily clear the Third World debt is also nauseating.

Another thing that gets my goat is magazines and television programmes that show people how the super-rich live. They're supposedly aspirational. They're not. How can a single parent living in a council flat in some godforsaken inner-city area ever aspire to have the kind of lifestyle that she sees plastered all over the 'celebrity' magazines that blight our newsagents? All these magazines do is dangle the impossible before the eyes of the most easily led and impressionable of people.

Having said that, considering the lack of talent of most of the people featured in these magazines, perhaps even the most stupid reader can harbour hopes of riches. After all, they could always try to marry a footballer. That seems to be a career choice for certain untalented young women in this day and age. Snag a brainless sportsman, spend his money and, before you know it, you'll be all over the gossip columns and glossy magazines. Maximum reward for so little effort: that seems to be the aspiration of most people these days.

But anyone who tries to work hard for a living, to earn money, to be a success, to use genuine talent … then God help them. We automatically assume they've done something illegal. We turn around and complain: 'He must have had help. He must have fiddled. Who gave him the money to do that?'

Instead, we should turn around and say: 'Well done. How can I do that?'

The way this country's going, though, too few people are asking that question. We're becoming a nation of mediocrity.

Another curse of our times.

I left school at sixteen, with barely any qualifications – purely and simply because the teachers hadn't thought it was worthwhile putting me in for the exams. I'd been told that I was too thick and probably wouldn't pass anyway. Despite that, I'm pretty sure I've got a CSE in woodwork, so all I can say is 'up yours' to the doubters who said I'd never achieve academic perfection.

Actually, I'm dyslexic, a condition that wasn't very well understood back then, so my problems with reading and writing were dismissed as mere stupidity. In fact, in my last year at school, the teachers largely ignored me. My mate Dick Pearce and I did mess about in the classroom and in that final year we were basically told that if we decided not to turn up then we shouldn't worry, because a blind eye would be turned. So that was what we did. I hardly went to school in my last year. I was happy and, presumably, so was the school.

Was I a problem teenager? I don't think so. I prefer to think that the fault was with the school system, which had an inability to cope with someone who wasn't the same as everyone else.

My first job when I left school was working for my

godfather, who owned a builder's yard in Ewell Village called Bean's. I began my working life as the delivery guy's mate, taking sand, cement, paving flags and anything else people wanted to expensive houses in Surrey so they could landscape their gardens. From that inauspicious beginning, I went on to a demolition team, knocking down buildings. One of these was a local pub, The Ship Inn. I spent a lot of my summer days leaning on shovels whistling at girls. I think that's part of a builder's job description.

It was hard work, but I enjoyed it and I was earning my first wage. A massive five pounds a week, to be precise.

However, my mother said: 'You can't spend your life doing this.'

I'm not quite sure what kind of career she expected me to pursue, but it obviously didn't entail wielding a sledgehammer eight hours a day. A friend of my mother's had a job at Harrods in London, so I was packed off there for an interview. I went, determined not to get the job if I could help it. At that time, I was quite happy being a builder's mate. The idea of working in some posh shop held no excitement for me whatsoever.

When I arrived, part of the interview involved an aptitude test, for which my dyslexia proved to be something of an unexpected bonus. The condition enables you to cope with abstract things quite easily so, almost to my dismay, I passed the test with flying colours and was taken on as a trainee buyer, despite the fact that I had no qualifications. (Though they didn't know that. Having gone there determined not to get the job, I'd seen enough of Harrods before and during the interview to convince me that working there might actually be a good idea. So when they asked me what O levels I had, I bluffed my way through it and, fortunately, they never asked to see written proof of my supposed academic achievements.) Like my schoolteachers before them, my employers at Harrods said I spoke very nicely. The accent I had was invaluable working there – it was just the sort of attribute my bosses loved.

I was placed in the toy department at Christmas and I enjoyed watching the debutantes who passed through that section of the store. I never managed to score with one, more's the pity – how different life might have been if I had.

I had a great time at Harrods. It was like one big party. No one else working there appeared to take it very seriously either. There seemed to be lots of 'resting' actors demonstrating toys or dressing up as Father Christmas. It must have been strange for them, playing Hamlet one week and then showing lots of whining little rich kids how to put Lego together the next.

During my time there, I would see all kinds of famous people wandering around buying things. Among these was the actor Frank Windsor (of Z Cars and Softly, Softly fame), whom I served one day while working in the men's toiletries department.

As I served him, I said excitedly, 'I've seen you in Z Cars.'

Z Cars was huge at the time. One of the biggest shows on television and he was one of its best-loved stars.

He looked at me a bit sniffily and replied: 'Have you really?'

I met him again a few years later when I was an extra on *Z Cars*. Subsequently, I've interviewed him on my TV and radio shows and shared that early memory with him.

I thought to myself what a great job he had. All he had to do all day was wander around Harrods being recognized and having tea – just like the hordes of other famous people I saw on an almost daily basis. It was then that I thought: 'I want to be famous.'

There was no great artistic drive behind my ambition, just the desire to be well known. How I was going to achieve my newfound goal, I wasn't sure. After all, I couldn't sing, dance, juggle, swallow swords, play the guitar or any other instrument. My options looked limited. My mother dissuaded me from being a dancer and she also had an opinion on the dramatic arts.

'You're not going into the theatre because it's full of poofs,' she insisted.

Those were the days when political correctness hadn't blighted and distorted everyone's vocabulary.

Around this time, however, I was suddenly faced with more pressing concerns than my budding career: the collapse of the family business. When S&R Whale went to the wall, as many small businesses did in the late sixties and early seventies, my dad was left jobless. It would have been bad at any time, but, as my dad was in his forties then, his prospects of finding another job seemed limited.

He had no choice. The house we lived in, where I'd been born and brought up, was sold.

For me, this was the end of the world. That house had been a haven, a sanctuary and a place of wonderful memories ever since I'd been born. The thought of now having to leave it was almost too much to bear. When I saw where we were moving to, I was even more concerned.

My dad sought salvation for our family by taking on the tenancy of a pub that he and my mum would run. He'd worked a few shifts at the local pub in Ewell, The Green Man, and he decided that that was what he now wanted to do.

Unfortunately, as far as I was concerned, the pub that he chose was in King's Cross, central London. The Harrison Arms was located in Argyll Square, a place then fairly notorious for its cheap hotels and 'ladies of the night'. The building itself was on the corner of Harrison Street and Seaford Street, next to a bombed-out church. We moved there in 1968.

Being uprooted from the leafy suburbs of Surrey to one of the roughest parts of inner London was little short of traumatic for me. True enough, I'd skived off school when I was younger and wandered around Soho, enjoying its various delights, but visiting London and living there were two different things. The city was a nice place to visit, but I didn't want to settle there.

At first, I refused to leave, insisting that I'd stay on in Ewell with my grandparents. Finally, however, I gave in and reluctantly moved into The Harrison Arms along with my mum and dad. In all fairness to him, my dad loved his newfound career. He flourished as landlord and my mum also adapted well to the move.

I was still working at Harrods at this time, but my newly acquired desire for fame was growing all the time. Ironically, it was through my dad's pub that I finally found a way to fulfil my ambition. The pub was owned by Watney's, one of the biggest breweries in the country, and they were looking for disc jockeys to run discos in their pubs. In the late sixties, this latest craze was just beginning. Watney's started a chain of clubs, all called The Bird's Nest, to cater to the new fad. Consequently, they had vacancies to be filled, playing music to the drinking masses. I got myself on to a training scheme in Twickenham to be a DJ in their clubs, and that was how my career started. Obviously, at that time, I had no idea that it was to take the direction that it did, but I thought the course might give me my crack at stardom.

I'd had a brief brush with what you could loosely call 'showbiz' when I was about fourteen or fifteen, in the shape of the Epsom Fair. This was held every year on the Epsom Downs during the week of the Derby, the famous horse race. The fair always arrived that week, and with it came the opportunity to earn some pocket money working on the stalls there.

The stall that all my schoolmates and I wanted to get jobs on was the striptease tent. For obvious reasons. Aside from the attraction of scantily clad women, music was always blasting out of the tent and I found the lure of pop music and half-naked women a very enticing combination, funnily enough. While the records were playing over the speakers outside the tent, someone would bang a large drum like the barker outside a Wild West show, literally to drum up trade. This was the job we all wanted so badly.

My friend Dick and I were paid five shillings to bang the drum outside the tent for three hours. As an added bonus, we would then slip, unseen, inside the tent, where we'd stand at the back and watch the strip show. It was a wonderful introduction to the world of the femme fatale.

Further initiation into the joys of the opposite sex

was gained when my friends and I took trips into Soho to visit Harrison-Marks. These trips started while we were still at school – sometimes taking place when we were supposed to be *in* school. Harrison-Marks were shops that sold saucy books, magazines and various appliances, much the same as Ann Summers stores do these days. All legal and above board, of course. The only difference was that, with the stricter censorship laws of the time, the models' genitals were airbrushed out. As far as we were concerned, though, looking at pictures of women with no genitals was better than nothing, so Harrison-Marks shops quickly became some of our favourite haunts.

My initial horror at being removed from the suburban tranquillity of Surrey to the hustle and bustle of King's Cross evaporated much more quickly than I'd imagined it would. As time went on, I began to see that there was far more to life than long walks on the Epsom Downs. London was a vibrant and exciting city and I rapidly became entranced by it.

I enjoyed being in and around the pub and I was sure that my quest for fame was well on its way. I continued with my training course for Watney's, wondering when I could become a full-time DJ. I was ready and waiting for fame to come knocking, thinking how wonderful it would be to be as recognizable as some of those well-known faces I'd seen around Harrods. I was convinced that once you became famous, you spent your time just walking round Harrods. My own time at that store had recently come to a rather inauspicious end when I was sacked from my job.

I was working in the food hall at the time and a commercial was being shot there. A huge shark had been displayed in the food hall for some kind of promotion that was being done (shark fin soup, I would imagine) and the makers of the commercial asked me to walk past the shark once or twice while they filmed.

'Wonderful,' I thought, 'in front of the cameras at last.'

Unfortunately, my employers didn't share my enthusiasm and I was told that, because I'd left my till unattended, my career in retail was not to be. I wasn't exactly devastated. I was sure that the training course for Watney's was about to propel me into my chosen industry. Without a doubt in my mind, I was convinced my time had come.

The Bird's Nest in Muswell Hill.

No, not the answer to a quiz question, but the place where I began my career as a DJ.

I got through the Watney's training course without any problems and the Muswell Hill gig was my first real DJ job. Three nights a week in there and two lunchtimes at The Bird's Nest in Waterloo. That venue was underneath Waterloo station and all sorts of businessmen came in there, some of whom I'd chat to in between putting on records. I'd never done anything like this before in my life. I didn't get paid, which was probably just as well. I was appalling. I wasn't sure what you had to do. My only experience of DJs had been listening to them on pirate stations like Radio Caroline. I had particularly liked and admired Johnnie Walker, Terry Wogan and Tony Windsor. However, after six weeks of training (once a week), I was assigned to The Bird's Nest and let loose on real-life punters.

I became, along with six or seven other guys, a resident DJ. It wasn't quite what I'd expected as we worked only a couple of hours a night, two or three nights a week.

However, one night while working there, I had an epiphany. As I was putting on a record, I actually managed to say: 'And now, back to 1966 and it's Marvin Gaye and "I Heard It Through the Grapevine".' I remember playing that record and thinking: 'Shit, that's what you do.' I finally felt like a real DJ. Everything seemed to click. Prior to that, I'd rambled on too much, over-embellished the introduction to the record, forgotten to mention details I felt I should have mentioned about the artist or the track ... but this time, everything was spot on. My delivery. My timing. Everything. I was helped by the fact that that particular record has a long instrumental intro. It gave me the chance to talk over the opening bars of music and get across the relevant information before Marvin burst into song.

After that, I became one of Watney's star DJs. You may ask why. Well, I'll tell you. Because I was bloody good. Even at such a young age, I was blessed with the kind of humility and self-appreciation I was to harness later in my career. Also, I had a voice for radio. I was blessed with that.

Watney's were certainly impressed. After less than a year, they offered me a job working in Sweden. In those days, it was quite a thing to be offered a job abroad working as a DJ and I was really excited by the prospect.

The gig they were offering was in a disco-pub run by an institute of some kind or another. It was based in Lund in Sweden. I went to meet the institute's representatives with some of the bosses from Watney's. We all convened at a mews house in Knightsbridge that was, funnily enough, just behind Harrods. Small world and all that rubbish. The institute was running the disco-pub and Watney's were to supply the DJ. Namely, yours truly.

Typically, by this time I'd settled comfortably into London life at my mum and dad's pub and I was really beginning to enjoy what went on around me. A diverse and interesting selection of customers used to come into the pub to drink, most notable of all being the villains who congregated in the public bar and the police who gathered in the lounge bar. Both sides would meet in the communal toilet and exchange information. A kind of lavatorial no man's land.

I'd also been seeing my girlfriend, Melinda (who, God help her, has been my wife for thirty-six years), for a while. We met in December 1968, when she was a final-year student at the London College of Fashion, at a disco in Oxford Circus. We'd both had dates, but both of us had been stood up. In an act of what I can only imagine must have been pity, Melinda agreed to let me buy her a drink. However, that particular night I was wearing a brand new leather jacket, the first one I'd ever bought, and, unfortunately, I'd left my wallet in one of the pockets when I'd deposited the coat in the cloakroom – so Melinda actually bought the drinks. It wasn't the most auspicious of starts to what was to become the most important relationship in my life.

At the end of the evening, I went to the cloakroom to collect my prized new leather jacket (and my wallet) – only to find that some bastard had taken the coat without having the correct ticket. I was furious, but looking back on it, I lost a leather jacket and gained Melinda. On balance, a fair swap.

Melinda went off to the Isle of Wight to work that Christmas, but we kept in touch and agreed to meet up in the New Year. We set a date, place and time, but to be honest I don't think either of us thought that the other would turn up.

Needless to say, both of us did. That date came and went and we agreed to meet again. This went on for a few months until one night, on the top deck of a London bus, I finally persuaded her to let me go back to her flat.

The inevitable happened. Our relationship developed quickly from that point on.

In fact, it developed so much that I returned to the pub one day to find my mother standing there looking stern.

'Well, you've done it now,' she told me.

'What do you mean?' I asked.

'I've had Melinda's mother on the phone,' Mum informed me. 'Melinda's pregnant.'

I hadn't known. Melinda hadn't even known. She'd gone to the doctors with a kidney infection and he'd actually felt the baby.

I felt that sinking feeling in my stomach. The quivering anus that you get when news of such earth-shattering importance is given to you suddenly afflicted me.

I was seventeen at the time. I was not ready to be a dad. I don't think I'd ever have been ready to be a dad, to be honest, but I knew that my mum expected me to face my responsibilities this time.

'You're going to have to forget about this stupidity now,' my mother continued. 'You're going to have to get yourself a real job.'

I didn't know what that meant, but I never got one!

I went to face my dad, who also knew. His reaction was a bit different.

'A bit of a mess, son,' he said. 'But don't you worry, we'll get through it.'

When Melinda told me herself, I said, with a typical man's detachment, 'Well, you're going to get rid of it, darling, aren't you?'

I simply couldn't cope with the situation. Pathetic, I know, but that's the way I was in those days. All I could think about was getting away. At that time, there was a huge stigma about having a child when you weren't married. I was quite content merely to run away from the problem.

What I didn't know was that both my own mother and Melinda's mother had been speaking to Melinda and they'd convinced her to have an abortion. The procedure was arranged, but as Melinda was several months pregnant, it wasn't going to be straightforward.

On the night before the operation, unbeknownst to me at that time, my dad went to see Melinda. He told her that if she wanted to change her mind, she could. He said something could be sorted out. This was the first time anybody had said to her that she could have the baby, which was what her heart was telling her to do. So, she got out of the hospital as fast as she could, and went back to her flat to work out what to do next. Of course, I wasn't being supportive through any of this. I was just being a bastard.

Melinda went back to college to do her final exams. The world in general still had no idea she was pregnant. I think she realized at that point that the only solution to the problem, now that she'd decided against an abortion, was to have the baby adopted.

Our child arrived in December. Melinda was induced and on 9 December 1969, at 8.15 a.m., our son was born.

He was named Michael Jason Maxted, the same initials as Melinda. I went to visit her and the baby, knowing that he was to be taken away. Despite my despicable behaviour and my lack of support for her, Melinda still agreed to see me. I arrived with my best friend, Julian. In those days, only fathers were allowed to visit on the first night. However, when the matron asked us who the father was, we both pointed to each other. In the end, she let us both in. Melinda was in a terrible state. Nevertheless, when the time came, she signed the necessary papers and the baby went off to a foster home.

Over the next few months, Melinda and I used to travel down to Littlehampton together, where our child now lived with his foster family. Those trips were heartbreaking, especially the return journey, knowing that we'd left him behind.

Finally, neither Melinda nor I could stand it any longer. We had to put an end to the torture. We had to have our three-month-old son back. Thankfully, the foster parents allowed us to take him back, as we hadn't yet signed the final documents putting him up for permanent adoption. They gave us their blessing and we headed to London with our son, whom we now called James because we liked the name (and you can't have two Michaels in the family!).

Of course, London wasn't going to be my home for long. With the Watney's job offer on the table, and the situation with James now happily resolved, I was about to head off to pastures new to take up my new post in Sweden. As usual, my dad had some words of advice for me. He suggested that, as I was about to go abroad to work, Melinda and I should get married. Melinda and I readily agreed.

So, the two of us went off to the King's Cross registry office one afternoon. We got married on 10 March 1971, in the time between The Harrison Arms closing in the afternoon and *Crossroads* coming on TV later that evening (it was my mum's favourite programme). There were only a handful of us at the ceremony: Melinda's mum, brother and granddad, my own parents, and the registrar. That was it. We went back to the pub for a makeshift party, and drank a couple of bottles of champagne upstairs in the kitchen.

We then got on with our lives.

I was now ready to go off to Sweden, thinking, perhaps foolishly, that I would make a life for us there and that Melinda and baby James would come and join me.

It didn't quite happen like that.

WHAT'S IN A NAME?

I was born Michael Whale.

I can hear some of you shouting now: 'Why does he call himself James Whale when his bloody name is Michael?'

You've probably been yelling it since reading chapter one.

It all goes back to when I first wanted to be an actor. In order to become a professional actor and make my mark on Hollywood, I was told that I would have to have an Equity card. No one was hired for TV, films, theatre or rep unless they had an Equity card.

I went to register my name one day, only to be told that there was already a Michael Whale registered. As in the film *Highlander*, 'there could be only one' as far as Equity was concerned.

How dare someone have the same name as me? Cheeky bastard. What made it worse was that this particular Michael Whale was some insignificant DJ at Radio 1. This man was preventing me from using my own name as an actor. When I became an international idol starring alongside the finest actors and actresses in Hollywood, I wouldn't be able to use my own name because this twat had already registered his.

But, of course, the history of entertainment is littered with famous people who, if they'd stuck with their original names, might not have become quite so famous. I mean, can you imagine the film *Top Hat* being such a success if it had starred Ginger Rogers and Fred Austerlitz (Fred Astaire's real name)? The posters wouldn't have looked so good for a start, would they? And if you'd walked into a record shop back in the seventies and seen the album *Goodbye Yellow Brick Road* by Reg Dwight, would it have had the same appeal? Elton John just sounds better, doesn't it?

So, I tried to come up with a catchy name that I could use in my career as an actor. I wasn't sure what name I should use instead. I toyed with 'Richard Lovelace' for a while, but decided against it. Probably just as well.

One morning, Melinda and I were walking down Harley Street on our way to the Equity offices. Melinda was pushing our son James along in his pushchair. The idea suddenly hit me. I knew what my name should be.

'I'm going to call myself James Whale,' I said, looking down at my son.

That was it. I'd simply steal my son's name.

And that was what I did.

He and I still laugh about it now. I suggested to him that he should change his name if he wanted to, but he decided not to. Quite right, too – why should he? After all, he had it first.

'I'm not changing it,' he always says. 'It's the name you gave me.'

So that's why you're reading the life story of James Whale – because I stole the name from my son.

Ironically, we'd settled on James's name to avoid having two Michaels in the family – then, thanks to my decision, we had two Jameses. The best-laid plans …

What I didn't realize when I made my choice was that there had been a very famous film director called James Whale back in the 1930s. He directed *Frankenstein*, *The Old Dark House* and *The Bride of Frankenstein*. Sixty years later, the part of James Whale the film director was played by Sir Ian McKellen in the film *Gods and Monsters* (1998). It was Sir Ian who pointed out the coincidence to me when he came into my studio one time.

So, to those in the know, I share my name with one of the most famous film directors of the Golden Age of Hollywood.

As far as my eldest son is concerned, I nicked his name.

Nutcases! There isn't a more appropriate word to describe the people I was working for in Sweden. The country was great. Cold, crisp, clean and sterile. Women were superior to men in all ways, as I remember. However, the institute I was working for, and its staff, were different propositions. My new colleagues made the end-of-the-world cult nutters look like well-adjusted human beings.

From day one, I remember thinking that the organization must be a front for something else (possibly criminal) because they didn't have many customers. They didn't even advertise for any. They made no attempt to increase their meagre profits. This disco-pub that I'd been hired to work in was as dead as a doornail. If I suggested things to make the place better or if I questioned their lack of enthusiasm, I was just told to get on with my work. I couldn't see how they were making any profit at all. I couldn't understand how these people had come to be involved in this kind of business. There had to be something else going on.

I became so convinced that this mysterious organization was up to something more insidious that I went off to the British embassy in Malmö to tell them who I was working for.

They didn't seem particularly interested in my apparently paranoid rants.

Still certain I was caught up in some kind of international espionage adventure, I went back to work. Unfortunately, my employers had heard of my trip to the British embassy and they weren't very happy. I was shown into a darkened room inside the club, where a number of them were waiting. It was like a scene from *The Godfather*. Five or six of them, including their leader, a female Gandalf with big tits, sat around like a hastily convened branch of the Spanish Inquisition (or perhaps that should be Swedish Inquisition) and proceeded to lay down the law to me.

In that room, I was told that if I didn't stop spreading malicious rumours about them and their organization, there would be severe consequences. I was told that they 'knew lots of people'. They didn't specify what kind of people, but it could have been anyone from international assassins to white slavers.

I was terrified.

They told me I would never work again. In fact, they told me they'd stop me getting an Equity card or, failing that, that I could end up building the Mao Tse Tung highway.

I was still reeling from these threats when they told me they were sending me to Copenhagen in Denmark for a couple of days. I immediately thought it must be to meet one of their torturers, but was relieved to discover that it was just because my visa was about to expire and needed renewing. They gave me some money to stay in a cheap bed-and-breakfast place and I was dispatched to

Copenhagen, where my passport was duly stamped and I was free to carry on working for these nutcases. To be honest, looking back on it, I don't know why I even considered continuing to work for them, but hindsight is always twenty-twenty and I had to earn a living somehow.

However, while I was in Copenhagen, I took advantage of my temporary freedom. I rang my dad (hoping that the phones weren't tapped) to tell him how miserable and terrified I was. I was in a foreign country and I was being threatened. I wasn't interested in working for these nutcases any more. All I wanted to do was go home.

In addition, determined to expose my employers, I visited the American embassy to tell them the same story I'd told the British embassy in Malmö.

The Americans were much more interested in my information, probably because I said I was convinced I was working for communists. I told them that my bosses wouldn't let me leave, that I couldn't get home and that the institute was virtually keeping me prisoner. Possibly a little bit of an exaggeration, but I was scared.

It turned out that the Americans had heard of this organization before and they were interested in them. I wondered if the CIA were already investigating these lunatics. The Americans asked me to go back and continue working. They also told me not to worry. That was a little like telling the owner of a blood bank not to panic just because Dracula was calling in for a visit.

I was sure that my life was in danger. Nevertheless, I returned to the club in Lund – only to find that an American had just started working there as a barman. Was he a CIA mole? Whether he'd been sent there because of the findings of the American embassy I have no idea, but this development served only to fuel my paranoia even more. It was like being caught up in some kind of spy adventure, but with none of the excitement, glamour or kudos.

Meanwhile, after receiving a series of frightened phone calls from me, my dad, back in England, had gone to the Foreign Office and told them of my plight. He also told them that the institute was holding my passport and refused to let me return to the UK. Fortunately, the Foreign Office were sympathetic. They paid for my plane ticket home and arranged for me to leave on a night flight from Sweden. I was finally going to get away from these mysterious people.

I was driven to the airport by one of the club's barmen, got on a plane late one night and flew back. Luckily, the British authorities allowed me to return without my passport, and I got another one from them at a later date. I don't think I've ever been so relieved to get out of anywhere in my life. I'd only been there for eight weeks, but it had seemed like an eternity.

Once I was safely back in England, I had to go along to the Foreign Office, not only to pick up my passport, but also for a debriefing on exactly what I knew about the institute. I was happy to tell the Foreign Office everything. When I'd relayed the story to them, they told me to go away, forget about everything and get on with my life.

I was just grateful to have the opportunity to get on with it. As far as I was concerned, if not for their intervention, I may well have been digging roads in China, if the nutters had followed through with their threat.

Moreover, I had other things in my life now. I was home, I was safe, I was relieved – and Melinda had a surprise for me. I was going to be a father for the second time.

For a young man who, at the time, wasn't even sure he wanted to be married, this was a major deal. I already had one child and was about to see the process repeated. Like James before him, Peter wasn't planned. Melinda and I were a lot less worried than we had been with the birth of our first son, though, because this time at least we were married. My first thought was that I had to find work – and fast. My rapidly expanding family would need supporting.

Watney's weren't very happy with the way I'd left them in the lurch by fleeing from the club in Sweden, so I didn't want to work for them any longer. I knew I'd have to branch out. In which direction, I had no idea.

All I did know was that when Melinda fell pregnant with our second child, she, James and I were living in one small room in The Harrison Arms. It wasn't easy, I can tell you. Melinda, quite sensibly, said that we had to find somewhere of our own to live. She got on the case and started looking into our options.

Upon returning from the clutches of the institute, I decided that acting was the way forward for me. I'd always been interested in drama, and now it seemed the best way for me to go so far as a career was concerned. I began taking acting lessons from a woman called Marion Ross, who was based in Russell Square, London, roughly ten minutes' walk from The Harrison Arms. Like every budding actor, I had visions of becoming a Hollywood star and threw myself into being a thespian. Like every budding actor, I quickly discovered that it wasn't the most lucrative of jobs, especially when you were starting out. I subsidized myself by working as a DJ anywhere that would hire me: birthday parties, weddings, and any other events. Anything that brought in some money to support Melinda and the family while I pursued my acting career.

After completing my drama lessons, I managed to get into repertory theatre at the Adelaine Jeunet Theatre, in East Grinstead – the home, I later discovered, of Scientology. In fact, there were so many followers of this unusual religion in the area that it was impossible to get digs unless you were a member. If Tom Cruise or John Travolta had been in rep in East Grinstead, they wouldn't have had any trouble finding somewhere to live, but that didn't apply to me, unfortunately.

Nevertheless, I took on the role of assistant stage manager at the Adelaine Jeunet. I used to sleep in the dressing room. It was horrendous and I managed to stand it for just four weeks. It was dull. It was boring. I left.

As the old maxim goes, though, as one door closes, another one opens. I was delighted when I landed myself a job as an actor in a play coming to the end of its run. It was only a month's work at the Oxford Playhouse, but I was grateful for anything. To bring in cash and increase my work experience, I also did lots and lots of work as an extra on various TV programmes around this time.

Not long before I went off to do the play in Oxford, Melinda and I were out shopping with James one day and we wandered into Topshop in Oxford Circus. As we walked around, listening to the sound of pop records, surrounded by people happily buying clothes, I thought: 'This is like a disco.'

An idea struck me. I thought that I could get a job there during the day, playing records, being a DJ inside the store. I could do a mini radio show within Topshop itself.

Even better, the shop was only a couple of hundred yards from Radio 1, which was housed, as it is today, in the BBC building in Langham Place.

'I ought to be on Radio 1 by this time,' I told myself.

Something that was never to happen, as it turned out, but at that time, for all budding DJs, Radio 1 was the pinnacle. The place to aim for. If I could get a job as a DJ at Topshop first, then surely I could use that as a stepping stone on my way into Radio 1.

I went to find the manager of Topshop. He was a man called Ralph Halpern, who was later to become famous in his own right when a Sunday newspaper plastered his 'five-times-a-night' sex exploits all over its front page. I told him of my idea and he said that they hadn't thought of anything like that. He told me to leave my phone number. To be honest, I didn't think much more about it and I went off to do the play in Oxford.

Once that was finished, I returned to London again, as ever wondering what I was going to do next as far as work was concerned. I hadn't been back that long when I got a call from Ralph, asking me if I'd like to come in and see him and have a chat about my idea for a radio station broadcasting inside Topshop. As I soon found out, Ralph loved the idea.

'We could have adverts for all the concessions,' he suggested.

There were lots of little designer boutiques inside the main store at that time, and it seemed a good way for them to advertise.

I was happy, Ralph was enthusiastic and everything went ahead. I set up a studio under the escalators (it's still there to this day) and Radio Topshop was born. A number of big names in radio went on to learn their trade there – including Chris Moyles, Gary King and Paul McKenna – but I was the one who actually came up with the idea and launched it. As it turned out, it was the first big step for me.

five **there's no business like show business**

From twelve noon until three in the afternoon, and then again from five until six in the evening. That was the beginning of my career in broadcasting, the launch of Radio Topshop. It was the first rung on the ladder and it felt very satisfying.

When I finished my afternoons at the Oxford Circus store, I'd wander up to a disco called The Sundown on Tottenham Court Road, opposite Centrepoint, and continue my DJ work there. I felt as if I'd arrived. I was earning good money, more than I'd ever made in my life at that stage, and things were looking up.

In the meantime, in one of the many instances when Melinda has taken care of the everyday details of life while I've been busily pursuing my career (for which I still thank her), my wife had managed to secure a council flat for our family of four (Peter had arrived almost two years after James, on 29 October 1971). Melinda had had to more or less camp out at social services, then, once she got to see them, she convinced them that we were being thrown out of my parents' place, and that the conditions for us and two children living in one room were unsanitary. She gave them a bit of a sob story, but, unfortunately, in order to get any reaction from bureaucrats, that's the name of the game.

Melinda's persistence got us a flat on the eighteenth floor of a high-rise block off Commercial Road in London. We were one of the first families to move into this block. It was brand new in 1972. To me, it looked like a pile of washing machines stacked up on top of each other, but it was to be our home.

One night, not long after we'd moved in, the wind was blowing so violently that we could feel the sides of the flat swaying – then it was as if the whole block was swaying in the wind. I was convinced the entire thing was going to collapse. I grew so scared that I rang my dad and asked him if he'd come and pick us up and take us back to the pub. In due course, Dad turned up and ferried us back to The Harrison Arms for the night. The next day, he gently persuaded us to give the tower block another go. The flat never blew away and the block never crumbled, fortunately.

We loved it in that apartment. It was huge – like a palace to us, compared to the one room we'd been living in at the pub. Our flat had wonderful panoramic views over London and we used to invite all our friends over for little dinner parties, just so they could stare out of the windows. We could see over the river, we could see St Paul's Cathedral. We could see for miles from there.

We were settled in our new home and I was thoroughly enjoying my work at Radio Topshop. One of the high points of my time doing the in-store show – aside from getting free records from all the record companies, of course – was the following experience. One day, two guys came to see me in the studio. One was a white chap with a huge Afro called Mike Leander; the other was a short, fat, bald guy called Paul Gadd. They brought me an acetate (a kind of demo tape, but for use on a turntable) of this record they'd just made. Little did I know it then, but that record was the start of a significant entry in the music industry's hall of fame.

'Would you like to give it a spin?' Mike asked.

I put it on and thought it was great. It didn't have much in the way of lyrics, but it was a really catchy tune.

'What's it called?' I wanted to know.

'"Rock and Roll",' they told me.

'What's the B-side?' I asked.

'That's going to be "Rock and Roll Part Two",' Mike informed me.

There was no band name on the acetate, just the titles of the two tracks. I played the record a few times in-store and the response was huge.

When Mike and Paul came back to see me a week or so later, I told them that people had been coming to the studio to ask where they could buy the song. It was a great party record and people wanted their own copies. Of course, it had still to be released, but the two guys were delighted with how well it had been received.

'What's the band called?' I asked.

Mike Leander wasn't sure. 'We're either going to call it Gary Glitter or Terry Tinsel,' he told me. 'We haven't decided yet.'

Thank heavens they chose Gary Glitter. Can you imagine songs like 'I'm the Leader of the Gang' being performed by a group called Terry Tinsel and the Tinsel Band?

Paul Gadd, needless to say, went on to become Gary

Glitter. He was the short bald guy who'd come in with Mike Leander when they first brought the acetate to me. I later discovered that they'd been looking for a singer to do the song, as Paul Gadd hadn't been the first choice. In fact, he hadn't been any kind of choice at all. He'd written the song with Mike, produced it and helped in the studio. It was only when no suitable singer could be found that Paul had taken on the persona of Gary Glitter.

As you already know, after they released the record, the song became a mega-hit.

To his credit, Mike Leander came down to the studio in Topshop one day. 'We really want to thank you for the support,' he said. 'This song has been a huge success and you started the buzz about it here by playing it in the store.'

So, as a reward, Mike asked if I wanted Gary Glitter to come and make a personal appearance in the store. Now these days, that kind of thing is commonplace, as the latest one-hit wonders are only too happy to appear personally at places like HMV or Virgin, but back in the early seventies, things like that never happened.

As Topshop had always been designed as a nightclub that sold clothes, I thought it was a great idea. I went along to see Ralph Halpern and told him that Gary Glitter was willing to appear in person at the store. The record was number one at the time, attracting massive media attention, so Ralph was delighted at the prospect.

'Yes, of course,' he said, enthusiastically. 'Get him to come down.'

Everything was set in motion. We arranged a date and time for Gary to appear. I played the record non-stop, to promote it and the personal appearance further.

Window displays and posters were created to advertise the – at the time – unique event. There was even a record store inside Topshop, which stocked plenty of extra copies of the single for people to buy. For a couple of weeks beforehand, everything in the store was geared to promoting the occasion.

I must admit, I was a bit worried in case no one turned up.

On the day of the event itself, Topshop got in extra fashion stock, because Ralph thought the place might be a little busier, even if people only wandered in out of curiosity. Early in the day, we set up a little stage, so there was somewhere for Gary to talk to me in full view of what I hoped would be his adoring public.

With all this frantic and rather costly preparation, I was even more worried that no one would be there.

The allotted time came and I got up on the stage, relieved to see that there were indeed people coming into the store – hopefully to see Gary Glitter, and not just to buy extra jeans and shoes.

Then my fears of no one turning up rapidly vanished. It was mayhem. No one had seen anything like this in a store, let alone a clothes store, before. So many people wanted to meet the singer of the number-one record. Massive numbers of fans were captivated by his glam-rock appearance and persona. Topshop was trashed. No one had thought about security, because no one had expected such a response. We had no crash barriers. Nothing. There were clothes going in all directions. People rushing to talk to Gary Glitter, desperate to speak to this new pop sensation.

It was such a frenzied reaction that I had to cancel the event halfway through, before too many people tried to tear off his sparkling stainless-steel-and-silver outfit. How he got out of there in one piece, I will never know.

Everyone who worked at the store was astonished at the power of this kind of event and, naturally, we went on to do many more.

It's easy to forget what a tremendous impact Gary Glitter actually had on the pop world given his later public shame, but I don't think that impact should be forgotten and I'm glad to say I was there at the beginning.

In fact, I actually introduced the first few Glitter live shows. Mike Leander rang me and told me that Gary Glitter was going out on tour.

'We want you to introduce him,' he said.

I was overjoyed. 'Great,' I thought. 'I'll be going out on stage in front of thousands of people.' I always was a bit of a ham actor.

My rock-and-roll dreams were quickly dashed, though, when I discovered that all the intros were to be recorded on a small tape recorder in Mike's office. Those intros were then plugged into the PA system and broadcast within whichever venue Gary Glitter was playing. So, his tour, and chapter of pop history, began.

The lights would be down, the crowd cheering with excitement ... then Gary Glitter would arrive on stage on a huge motorbike. He did that at every arena he played, whipping the audience into hysteria. The little bald guy I'd first met in Topshop would appear in his dazzling costume, tottering on huge stack heels and wearing a jet black wig, now transformed into this alter ego who was taking the charts by storm.

Just before the show started, a voice would boom out over the PA.

'Ladies and gentlemen, it's Gary Glitter.'

That voice was mine.

Even though I was doing very well at Radio Topshop, doing DJ stuff in clubs and earning very good money, I was (predictably for me) not entirely settled. I was still an actor at this time too and I was still drawn to TV. Television was the place to be in the early seventies – at least, it was the place I thought I wanted to be.

I was still getting work as an extra and featured on lots of TV shows, *Z Cars* particularly. I also appeared regularly on *Doctor Who*, and on the comedy series *Bless This House*, which used to star Sid James. I had small walk-on parts in all these programmes and thought that I might yet be discovered during one of these split-second appearances.

It was during a stint as an extra that I met one of my oldest friends, Peter Perry. I met him when we were both playing monsters in *Doctor Who*. It was strange because while I thought I wanted to break into television, Peter was more anxious to do some radio. He actually rang me one day and said: 'Can you get me into radio?'

'What do you want to do?' I asked him.

'I want to be a DJ,' he told me.

'No, you don't,' I said to him. 'What we really need is people to sell in radio.'

Advertising space and that kind of thing, I meant. As it turned out, Peter was very successful at that, and he went on to become managing director of Allied Radio in the south.

While all this was happening, commercial radio was beginning to establish itself in this country. LBC was the first ever British commercial station, but, at the time, it was just a talk-radio station. I was actually interviewed by LBC for a feature, because I was the country's first in-store DJ.

During that interview, I had an epiphany. Suddenly, all my acting aspirations were shelved. I realized that I wanted to be on the radio and I didn't mean playing records in Topshop's basement. I wanted to be broadcasting to millions of people from a studio, speaking about subjects that interested me and, hopefully, also interested the people listening.

That was what I really wanted to do. I loved it.

There's a world of difference between playing records and chatting about what's a hit in the pop business, and actually discussing important subjects that millions of listeners want to hear about and also discuss. I suppose it's the difference between a DJ and a presenter, really.

So, freshly infected with this desire to be a broadcaster (excuse my lapse into pretension there), I went for interviews with a number of radio stations.

One of these came about due to a guy who used to come into the Topshop studio a lot, always boasting about how well he was doing and what a great DJ he was on Manx Radio. I was quite pally with him and I was in his office one day when he said: 'I've just got an interview with a brand new commercial radio station, it's going to be huge.'

'Where is it?' I wanted to know.

'Newcastle. I think I've got the job.'

He was so insufferably sure of himself and the fact that he thought he'd got this job that I could think of only one thing to do. I chatted to him, got all the details, then I went home and got in touch with this radio station – and got myself an interview. The station was Metro Radio, which wasn't yet on the air. I went all the way to Newcastle and did a quite ridiculous audition in a disco in Pink Lane.

Halfway through the tryout, the turntables stopped working. Broke down. One of the jingles I had to play also broke. I just stopped, turned to the people auditioning me and said: 'Sorry, guys, it's not working.'

They looked gormlessly at me.

'That was part of the audition,' they insisted. 'We wanted to see what you'd do if there was a crisis on air.'

'I'm not on the air,' I responded. 'I'm in a nightclub, pretending to be on the radio and the equipment's just broken. If I was in a studio, I'd deal with it.'

They weren't impressed. I didn't get the job.

I headed back to London, still wondering how I could break into this wonderful world of commercial radio. It was 1974 and I still hadn't got my own show on the radio. 'Something's wrong here,' I thought. 'How much longer am I going to have to wait?'

Not put off by the cack-handed audition I'd had in Newcastle, I rang the guy who was running Metro Radio with a new idea that I'd come up with. I thought I could be the London correspondent for Metro, and all the other local radio stations that were opening up all over the country. I was living in London. I was on the spot. I could do interviews with all the well-known people in the capital and those interviews could then be broadcast locally.

I spoke to a guy at Metro called Paul Lewis, who was programme controller at the time.

'I'm glad you rang,' he said.

'Why's that?' I wanted to know.

'Someone's just dropped out. Do you want to come and work for us?'

I couldn't believe it. For years, I'd been trying to get into radio. I was twenty-three, I thought life had passed me by – then suddenly, because of a chance phone call, I was being offered a job in the industry I wanted to make my living in.

'Are you serious?' I asked, still somewhat taken aback.

'We're going to put the job offer in writing,' he told me. 'It'll consist of doing some of the early evening news and continuity announcing.'

Continuity announcing basically involved sitting in a studio introducing other shows on Metro. One of these was a kids' show called *Timber Tops*. It was bollocks. No one listened to it, but part of my job was to announce shows like this. The fact that the guy who wrote *Timber Tops*, Ken Blakeson, went on to write for *Coronation Street* is by the by.

The people who ran Metro in the early days were TV people and they were going to run it as a TV station without the pictures. I thought they knew nothing. They seemed to have no idea. That was lucky for me because I'm sure, if they had, they'd never have taken me on.

Yet they did take me on, and I was also given my own two-hour show between ten o'clock and midnight. All of Metro's shows after six o'clock in the evening, excepting mine, were recorded, so I would link them in as they were all on tape, and then I'd do two hours live, playing laidback music to help people sleep. I'd close the station down at midnight.

That was the job description I was given.

'What's the contract offer?' I wanted to know.

'We'll offer you three months initially,' Paul Lewis said, 'and we'll pay you fifty pounds a week.'

I didn't even think about discussing it with Melinda first.

'Send the paperwork down,' I told him.

CRIME AND PUNISHMENT

I am getting sick and bloody tired of the lack of discipline in society.

You can't smack your children. You can't tell them off. You can't do anything. We have such a lack of discipline in this society, it would be ridiculous if it wasn't so bloody alarming. The good people of this country don't want to have to live in fear of their lives. They don't want to have to walk down their high streets running the gauntlet of ill-educated, stupid people. They want to be able to feel free to go about their business.

In my opinion, therefore, criminals *have* to be brought to account. If that means building more prisons, then let's build more prisons, but I don't think we need that. Instead, what should happen is that prison should be made the most appalling, disgusting and vile place – so that once you've been there, you never, *ever* want to go back.

Bread and water would be great. Beatings regularly.

I don't care what all the do-gooders say. People who won't speak to me any more, by the way. The people from Friends of Prisoners or the Penal Reform group. Prats like that.

A prisoner – a murderer at that, who kicked a man to

death – recently tried to sue the government because they wouldn't allow him and his wife to continue with IVF treatment while he was inside. His audacity beggars belief. And I ask you, what kind of woman would want to have the spawn of a murderer anyway? I think the women who marry men while they're in prison want locking up too. Years ago in America, when the serial killer Ted Bundy was on trial for the murder of over thirty college girls, he had sackloads of proposals from women wanting to marry him. What exactly were those women looking for? Frankly, Bundy must have possessed an amazing sense of humour. That is the thing that women supposedly prize most highly in a man, isn't it?

One of the Kray twins got married while in prison. So did Charles Bronson, the most dangerous man in England. This should not have been allowed. Prison should mean prison – segregation from decent society.

But what am I saying? Let's face it, we all know prison is a joke these days. It's no wonder our prisons are full to bursting when the do-gooders are showering criminals with PlayStation2 machines and all the occupational therapy money can buy. What kind of punishment is it to these convicts to be locked up with all the mod-cons they could possibly desire?

Meanwhile, law-abiding people go without. It'd be laughable – if it wasn't so fucking wrong.

I say, let's build huge treadmills in prisons. Everyone's green at the moment, or always going on about alternative power sources, so let the prisoners provide the power. Let the bastards do something useful while they're inside. Stick them on these treadmills for eight hours a day. Let them walk round like a hamster on a wheel, generating electricity that we can then put back into society.

I don't see it happening, though. Someone, somewhere – probably in Brussels, the base of the European Parliament that is undoubtedly now our lord and master, regrettably – is probably drafting some new law so that these poor prisoners are protected from such innovative ideas.

As usual, the criminals are mollycoddled, and the rest of us pay the price. Bloody typical.

In 1974, I was earning a lot of money from all my different jobs. As well as the Topshop post, I was also doing a stint as the DJ at The Chelsea Drugstore. This was a very fashionable and trendy club on the King's Road. I managed to get Melinda a job there as a go-go dancer. She used to dance in a cage. You could say it was good practice for her, because being married to me must have felt like being in bloody prison at times.

When I spoke to Metro Radio and agreed to take their job for fifty pounds a week, I was looking at a huge cut in wages. Wages that I needed to support Melinda and the children. Nonetheless, I was prepared to give it all up to go to Newcastle on a three-month contract. I'd also been offered a job at Radio Hallam in Sheffield, by the man who was then managing director, a man called Keith Skews, but I thought, for various reasons, that I'd go with Metro.

I had no guarantee of a job after the three months were up. If I left London, it would likely spell the end of the lucrative regular income that I was enjoying, but all I could see was the offer of a job in radio. Something I wanted so badly, I was prepared to take the gamble.

The thing was, I wouldn't just be gambling with my own future, I'd also be gambling with Melinda's future and the future of our two children. But I was determined. Nothing was going to stop me.

When I think about that particular decision and, unfortunately, too many others like it that I've made during my life, I am amazed that Melinda ever stuck by me. I don't deserve her. I didn't then and, sometimes, I don't think I do now.

Just as Melinda was settled somewhere, I would throw a spanner in the works. I'm not proud of myself for that.

I finally spoke to Melinda about the job offer from Metro Radio.

'What do you think?' I asked.

'You must do it,' she said.

Yet again, she supported me in my own selfish desire to achieve what I wanted in life.

I never mentioned the fact that I'd already decided to take the job anyway.

The wheels were set in motion. Melinda, James and Peter were to stay behind in London for the next three months, while I got myself sorted in Newcastle. Moving meant that we'd eventually have to give up the flat in London, the one that Melinda had struggled so hard to get. This huge two-bedroom palace of ours with its massive lounge, kitchen, dining room and bathroom, with our panoramic views over London. However, in the two years since we'd moved in, when everything had been pristine, the block had become like a tenement. Other people who'd moved in hadn't treated the place with the same respect that we had and it wasn't a good place to bring up kids. The lifts smelled of urine. You could see rats running about on the ground floors. In truth, I was pleased to be moving. I packed up all my worldly possessions that I thought I'd need and headed to the North-East.

I got off the train in Newcastle, to be picked up by a taxi that took me to Metro Radio. The taxi was driven by a woman. I was flabbergasted. Women didn't drive taxis, did they? Not in London, they didn't. The taxi driver thoughtfully showed me where a number of murders had taken place as we drove along. How caring of her.

The radio station itself was in a little place called Swalwell. It was in the back of beyond, with coal tips opposite the radio station. It was cold and depressing. To reach the hellhole of a building in which the station was housed, you had to drive down a muddy track with huge piles of coal on either side. The air smelled like a slag heap – you could virtually see the specks of coal dust floating in the air. I was worried about breathing in too deeply in case I inhaled coal dust. It looked as if you could have got silicosis just from walking around outside. The place looked terrible and I felt terrible.

I'd left the bright lights of London, given up all my contacts there, left behind my wife and two children – and for what? For this dump?

I just wanted to go home, but I didn't even have a base in Newcastle yet to call home. I had nowhere to stay at that time. The radio station had said they'd find me digs. I was so homesick, and I hadn't even been there a day. I missed London, I missed Melinda and I missed the kids – but I'd made my choice.

I got into the radio station itself and things didn't improve much. It was a building site. I was confronted by a man who looked like a farmer: a man called Neil Robinson, who was the chief engineer at Metro. The first time I saw him, he was wheeling a wheelbarrow into what was going to be the main reception of the radio station … when it was finally completed. There were piles of cement and bricks everywhere and the air was full of dust. It looked as if I'd walked on to the set of a war film.

'Who are you?' Neil asked.

'I'm James Whale,' I told him. 'I'm a DJ.'

'Not at the moment, you're not,' he said. 'Dump that stuff, roll up your sleeves and help me shift this.'

I was almost in tears. The last time I'd been surrounded by this much debris was when I was working at the builder's yard after leaving school. Trying to overcome my disappointment, I helped him move the rubble he'd indicated.

I hated Metro Radio – and I hadn't even done my first show yet.

The next challenge was for me to get to know the rest of my colleagues. I met the programme controller and a few other people, including the guy who was doing the morning programme, a man called Don Dwyer, a little wrinkled old Aussie. Another workmate was Giles Squire, a young fresh-faced chap who was a bit full of himself. Despite this, he and I ended up sharing a house together, until I could find somewhere for my whole family to live.

Unsurprisingly, Metro's launch was postponed, mostly due to the fact that the building wasn't completed. This did have its good side, though. Apart from the fact that I was getting paid even though I wasn't working, it also meant that I lived up in Northumberland for quite some time. All the DJs were regularly taken around in minibuses so that we could get to know the area. By the time we went on the air, which was about three months later, I knew more about the North-East than most Geordies.

Some of my colleagues decided to try to put on Geordie accents to make themselves more acceptable to the locals, but I never did. I never felt the need and I also dislike trying to be something that I'm not.

What I discovered during those three months was that there was something about the North-East, and particularly Northumberland, that I loved.

Melinda came up for a couple of weekends and she realized that it would be a great place to bring up the kids. We decided we didn't want to live in the town. Despite our years in London, we were never really townies. We preferred to live in the country. Luckily, we found exactly what we were looking for in a place called Prudhoe, an old mining community about fifteen miles outside Newcastle. We discovered a little mid-terrace miner's cottage on a hillside with fabulous views over the Tyne valley. With a little help from my grandmother, we bought the cottage for £6,500.

By this time, my initial three-month contract with Metro was up, but they offered me another six months. I was delighted. I was enjoying doing the night-time show myself. The station had given up the idea of recorded programmes, so I didn't have to do any more bloody links. I could just concentrate on my own show – and I was already hitting the headlines. A guy called James Stannidge started on Piccadilly Radio in Manchester at around the same time as I started on Metro, and the national newspaper the *Sunday People* ran a big article about which one of us was the rudest man on British radio. To which I was happy to concede the title, because I've never considered myself to be rude on the air.

For the management at Metro, however, things weren't going so well. Paul Lewis and his father, Bruce, were in overall charge of the station, but what didn't help the organization, as far as I could see, was that they had an old headmaster running some of the programmes, and he apparently had no idea about radio at all. The board of directors wanted to get rid of everyone, including me.

I remember Bruce Lewis sitting in his office refusing to go, virtually barricading himself inside. I felt sorry for him, obviously – the guy gave me my first break in radio.

Mind you, I suspect the only reason he did give me my first break was because he knew as much about radio as I did.

This upheaval all happened within the first six months of me working for Metro. It was something of a baptism of fire, but at least Melinda and I had been able to get on the housing ladder with the cottage in Prudhoe, so not everything was looking bleak.

In fact, life was pretty good: we were in our early twenties, we had two healthy sons, we had a foot on the property ladder, and I had a job on the radio – a job I managed to keep, despite the aforementioned 'Metro massacre' – in which I got to interview all kinds of famous people.

In those days, so-called celebrities actually bothered to tour the regional radio stations, instead of just sitting in some flash hotel in London, doing all their interviews down the line from the BBC. People with a film, book, record or TV series to promote seemed more willing to put in the promotional legwork; something else that has changed.

As it happened, I became very well known in that small corner of the North-East for doing the legendary (well, legendary in the North-East) late-night phone-in show *Nightowls*; a show that still bears that name to this day. It's still very successful because it's a simple idea. Basically, it's chatting to people on the phone, having a bit of a laugh. As with so many things in life, radio should not be overcomplicated. There's no need for think tanks and the views of university graduates or demographic researchers. Radio is about people. The listeners. It was when I was at Metro and it still is to this day.

At Metro, I used the very simple formula of speaking to members of the public as if they were human beings, not treating them like idiots and talking down to them. If you want to do a good talk show on the radio, just imagine you're leaning on your garden fence. Radio talk shows are the modern garden fences. They're where people chat. People used to talk to each other like that face to face years ago – now they do it over the airwaves. The radio talk show is the public bar of the nation. That was the way I always viewed my show when I was doing it for Metro and, fortunately, people responded to that approach.

I got involved in a number of publicity stunts during my time with that station, including breaking the world record for kissing the most women in a given time. It was all for charity, I hasten to add, and I put myself through the agony of kissing 4,049 girls in just eight hours. The things I do for publicity. I raised over a thousand pounds for charity – and felt as if my lips were going to fall off when I'd finished. I'm grateful to Melinda for letting me practise on her.

I also decided to do a skydive, once again for charity. This didn't work out quite as well to begin with. I'm not a superstitious man, and I don't usually take much notice of things like horoscopes, but a friend of mine who was an astrologer, Joan Porter, warned me that, around the time the jump was scheduled, my stars said I was passing through 'an accident-prone period'. Normally that kind of warning wouldn't have bothered me, but for some reason, this time it did. To this day, I don't know why. I'd had eight weeks of training to get me ready for the jump, but I couldn't get that piece of information out of my mind. Accident prone, at thirty thousand feet? There was no way I was risking it. I know that lots of people must have thought my decision to postpone the jump was down to cowardice, but it wasn't. All I wanted was a fine day and assurances from an astrologer that the accident-prone phase had passed. Needless to say, it eventually did.

One of the more bizarre things I was called on to do by the programme director of Metro was a broadcast from a submarine. The reason for this was that the submarine had just been adopted by the Northumberland town of Blythe, a small mining town on the north-east coast with a port. Metro arranged for me to be picked up by a Sea King helicopter, then winched down on to the casing, the deck of the submarine. Off I went with my producer and we did the show. It was an incredible experience being on this vehicle that was shaped like an amazingly large and long cigar, knowing that it was about to set out to sea for a three-month tour.

We did most of the programme while the sub was moored, but also experienced a little bit of movement. It was a lovely crisp winter's afternoon as we left the port. I was interviewing the captain, George, at the top of the conning tower. The sub wasn't allowed to submerge with civilians on board, so we simply steamed out into the North Sea for a couple of miles. The Sea King was then booked to come back and lift me from the conning tower while the sub disappeared beneath the grey, churning waves of the sea. We got the call that the chopper was en route, five minutes away from picking up me and my producer. The two of us dutifully climbed a little further down the conning tower to wait. One of the things I'll never forget was that the inside of the tower was covered with barnacles and smelled very strongly of seaweed. With the sun sinking in the west and the smell of the sea so strong in my nostrils, I felt like an extra in a war movie.

Twenty-five miles out into the North Sea, the Sea King arrived to winch us off. The noise was incredible as its rotors cut through the air. First my producer was hauled up into the chopper; then I followed. It was an experience I'd never have had had I pursued a normal career. I don't think there's much call for helicopters when you're working in Harrods.

All these opportunities combined made me certain – for the time being – that I was working exactly where I wanted to be. The only question seemed to be: how long would it last?

During my time at Metro Radio, I was lucky enough to make some great friends and meet some fascinating people. Throughout the seventies, Melinda and I became very friendly with a couple called Brian and Carol Johnson, whom we met because I interviewed Brian on my programme a few times and we seemed to have a lot in common. Brian used to pop into the radio station occasionally, and he and I would go out for a drink.

Brian was the lead singer of a very well-known band in the seventies called Geordie. A kind of North-East version of Slade. They were hugely popular, particularly in the North-East. Brian was a very rugged ex-paratrooper who, strangely enough, turned to music. Hardly a logical progression, I know, but it worked for him.

In the course of my years on Metro Radio, Geordie suffered a bit of a decline, touring working men's clubs and pubs and struggling to get a record deal, having been dropped by their last company, Red Bus Records. Brian established a little business on the quayside in Newcastle, putting sunroofs into cars, to help support himself while the musical side of his life wasn't going great guns.

One night in the late seventies, Brian walked into the studio, not to be on the show, but just to have a chat with me while I was off-air. I asked him what was going on.

'I've been asked to go and do an audition,' he told me in his broad Geordie accent, 'for this band in London, but I don't know whether or not it's worth going down.'

So, the pair of us had a long conversation about whether or not it was worth Brian travelling all the way to London for this audition. He'd never really heard of the band and wasn't very enthusiastic. I asked him what the band was called.

'AC/DC,' he said.

Yes, *the* AC/DC. They'd already had massive album success with *Dirty Deeds Done Cheap* and hit singles like 'Whole Lotta Rosie'.

'I think you should do it,' I told him.

'But my car business is doing really well,' he complained.

Nevertheless, he finally decided to go and I gave him some money for the train fare. The rest, as they say, is history. Brian got the job and sang vocals on one of the biggest selling rock albums of all time, *Back in Black*. He's with AC/DC to this day. A multimillionaire. I occasionally see him being interviewed on television; I've never spoken to him since that evening at Metro.

Meanwhile, due to the success of my radio show and my limited notoriety in that part of the world, I was asked, by a man called Andy Hudson, to compere a series of events at the 1976 Newcastle Festival. Andy came up with the idea that I should do a series of live chat shows on stage at the University Theatre in

Newcastle. For this, I was paid the princely sum of twenty-five pounds. One of these shows involved interviewing the legendary Diana Dors. She was, at that time, a very famous woman. She'd been in films and on TV for years. A big, impressive and very sexy woman. I duly did the interview that afternoon, but then, because her train didn't leave for London until nine that night, I was entrusted to look after her until I could drop her off safely at the station. After we'd done the chat show, it was about six o'clock, so I said to her: 'What would you like to do now?'

'Perhaps we could go and get something to eat,' she suggested.

That was fine with me. The two of us went off to an Indian restaurant called the Koinoar in Newcastle's Bigg Market. The waiters inside got very excited when they saw her because she had such presence, and she was wearing the most amazing jewellery and full evening dress. The only thing was, these waiters were suffering from a case of mistaken identity. They kept calling Diana 'Doris'.

Diana finally leant over to me and said: 'James, I think that they think I'm the other blonde.'

'Who?' I asked. 'Marilyn Monroe?'

'No, Doris Day.'

Indeed, the waiters were absolutely convinced that she was Doris Day, the American actress. Apparently this happened quite a lot. I'm sure Doris Day frequently got mistaken for Diana Dors, too. Who knows? At the end of the meal, Diana sportingly stood up and said: 'Would you like me to sing "Surrey with the Fringe on Top"?'

At that point, the other people in the restaurant got up and applauded her. Showbiz, eh?

So, life was good in the North-East. In time, we moved to a bigger house with some land. Melinda, as well as being able to buy a horse, whom we named Ebony, also found a couple of abandoned goats. She looked after them and bred them and we ended up with a small herd. Life ticked along comfortably for us.

It was late in 1979 when I got a phone call early one morning from my mum.

'Michael,' she said. 'I'm afraid your dad died last night.'

I did what I usually do in times of great stress. I went out and washed the car.

The news hit me hard, but I was still determined to go into the studio and do my show that night. However, the people at Metro insisted I take some time off.

'Take the week off,' they told me.

'I don't want to,' I protested. 'I might need next week off, but not this week.'

I thought I'd be better off working, but I finally agreed to take some time out.

It was bizarre. I'd only phoned my dad the previous night. He and my mum had been planning to move up from London to run a pub in Newcastle. They'd spent a few weekends with us and I'd convinced them that the North-East was a wonderful place to live. Everything was sorted. They'd even spoken to the brewery about taking over a place. I'd wanted to speak to my dad about something, so I'd rung him the night before.

'He's not feeling too well,' my mum had said. 'He's gone upstairs to have a sit down. Ring him tomorrow.'

I didn't think anything more of it until I left the radio station that night. As I was about to walk out, I turned to the security guard and said: 'I think my dad's going to die.' I don't know what made me say that. He'd never been ill. He was always a healthy bloke.

Then, the following morning at seven o'clock, my mum rang me to give me the terrible news that my dad had passed away.

A few days elapsed and I went down to London. I ran the pub for a week. It was one of the hardest weeks of my life. The stream of well-meaning people coming in and saying, 'Where's your dad, then?' didn't help, but they weren't to know. I helped sort out the funeral arrangements. I also moved my mum back to Wales, where she'd been born. She just wanted to go back to her roots after Dad died.

I know this sounds bitter, but I'm sure anyone else who's suffered the loss of someone close will understand when I say it took me about two years to stop looking at people in the street and thinking: 'Why are you alive?' I just wanted it to be anyone else but my dad who was dead. I began to detest people who'd done bad things and were still living. Why the fuck should they carry on enjoying life when my dad was dead? My dad, who never hurt anyone in his life, was gone, and yet there were hundreds of thousands of scumbags walking the streets who could, who *should*, have been in his place. Perhaps it's part of the grieving process. I was only twenty-eight at the time and I felt like I'd been robbed of my dad.

If I have a regret, it's that my dad died before I'd achieved some of the things I set out to. I felt that I was always ringing him up to say, 'Dad, can you lend me a few bob?' instead of calling him to say, 'Hey, Dad, let's go away for a weekend' or 'Let's go out and have a meal.' I'm sure a psychiatrist would look for some kind of Freudian meaning in those thoughts, but to me it's as simple as having wanted to share my success with the man who helped bring me into this world.

I couldn't settle much after his death. Even though Melinda and I had, by that time, moved into another house in a little village called Mickley, I was restless.

'I want to move, I want to leave,' I said to her one day. 'I want to do something else.'

I'd been on the radio since I was twenty-two and now, seven years later, I thought I'd accomplished everything I wanted to. At least, in my mind at the time, I had. I wanted something new to do.

As usual, Melinda understood.

I opened up a trade magazine and saw a job advertised on BBC Radio Derby. I wanted it. I thought it would be the perfect launch pad for the next stage of my career. I rang up and they asked me to go down and audition.

I got the job, which I'm sure was down to my eloquent speaking voice, once again. The interviewers seemed delighted with the way I said 'BBC Radio Derby', enunciated with perfect diction and the kind of gravitas that the BBC thinks it deserves. It wasn't the night job I'd had at Metro, but the mid-morning show, broadcasting from ten in the morning until one in the afternoon. The show was called *Lineup*. I hated it. It was the worst kind of local radio. It involved interviewing women from the WI about jam-making and charity things – certainly not what I'd been used to.

I moved into digs in Derby. Yet again, I left Melinda on her own. She was stuck in Newcastle with the kids, the dogs, the horse and a herd of goats. I don't know how she put up with it. As always, she never moaned, she never complained. Not once. She just got on with it. In fact, the morning I got the job she came into the bedroom and said: 'Good morning, Mr BBC man.'

What a woman.

The job paid me half what I was getting at Metro. We had a huge mortgage on the house in Mickley, but I still took it. We couldn't pay the mortgage for a year. However, expecting to move to Derby, we put the house on the market, so the bank never had any problems with us. The money we owed, they told us, would simply come off the price we got for the house when we finally sold it.

But by the time I'd worked at Radio Derby for just a short while, I hated the BBC and everything it stood for. In my opinion, the BBC wastes money because it doesn't actually have to earn it, thanks to the licence payers. It treats people like scum. It's supercilious and assumes it, and its employees, are better than everyone else.

Every day I left Radio Derby after my show, I threatened to quit.

I had thought I was going to be huge because I'd imagined that working for the BBC would be a stepping stone to television shows like *Pebble Mill at One*. After my dad had died, my restlessless had fused into a temporary desire to be a 'serious broadcaster'. I wanted to make my dad proud, even if he wasn't around any more to see it, and in my grief I thought that this would be the best way forward. I'd hoped that the BBC would facilitate this new desire. But it never happened. I soon came to my senses over the worthiness of 'serious broadcasting' and the pretension that went with it: a few months working at the BBC were enough to get me over that particular phase.

To keep myself sane, I went out and found some work doing voiceovers. I travelled around the country recording commercials. I earned more money doing one thirty-second commercial than I did working for a week on the radio.

One day in 1981, I was at a recording session at a fairly new radio station called Radio Aire, in Leeds, when the boss of the station came and found me. The guy who ran Radio Aire was called Geoff Sagerson. He was a big bloke with a big bushy beard. He looked like a cross between Santa Claus and Blackbeard the pirate. A really nice guy.

'Why don't you come back to commercial radio?' he asked. 'We're just about to go twenty-four-hour and we need someone to do the ten-o'clock-until-one window.'

He made me an offer that was too good to refuse.

Despite the fact that I'd wanted to do something different, despite my misgivings about working on the late-night slot again, and regardless of the strain it might put on my relationship with Melinda, there was only one answer I could give.

I took the job.

At the beginning of the eighties, I gleefully left the BBC – which, I'm sure, wasn't sad to see the back of me either – and I went to Radio Aire in Leeds. We finally managed to sell the Mickley house at the same time, which was convenient. For a couple of weeks, while all the paperwork was going through, I stayed in Leeds with one of the other DJs on Radio Aire, a lovely guy called Alex Lester. Alex let me have a room in his house on Argie Road in Leeds. It was a back-to-back terraced house, the kind of stereotypical northern dwelling you always see in films and on TV.

Meanwhile, Melinda and I began looking for a house with some land to accommodate our horse and our goats and our dogs. I was more like James Herriot than James Whale. Luckily, we soon found a little cottage on the side of a main road. It was far too small, but it had a good piece of land for the animals, so we bought it. That's where we began our Yorkshire experience.

I didn't expect us to stay there for very long, but we actually ended up living there for eighteen years. I just assumed that with my naturally itchy feet and habit of losing interest in things quickly, we'd be moving on again in a couple of years.

I should have been a gypsy, really. I've never been able to settle in places easily and, if I do, I tend to want to move on. Perhaps that old expression about a rolling stone gathering no moss is true in my case.

The main problem with the house in north Yorkshire was that it was in the middle of nowhere, but on a very main road. However, we got used to the traffic thundering past and the animals seemed happy enough. Harrogate, in which we spent more time than Leeds, is a great town. A good place to bring up kids (though the boys both went to school in Ripon because that was nearer to the house) and the people were friendly.

One of the things I did when we moved to Yorkshire was to take up falconry. Don't ask me why, I have no idea, but we lived in the middle of the country and the farmers nearby were quite happy for me to exercise my bird of prey over their land. I think I'd always wanted to be one of those people who could just look at an animal, say a word and make the animal respond. I wish people could be trained to respond like that too – it would make life much easier.

My eldest son, James, who was twelve or thirteen at that time, was very keen on country sports, and the interest that we both shared in outdoor pursuits led me to contact a falconer who lived just outside Bradford. James and I spent many happy afternoons with this man, learning about falconry; learning how to make the jesses and the hoods and the muse, which is the place where you keep your hawk. My own bird (Esmeralda, not Melinda) was far too well fed by me to be bothered about catching rabbits, but my son and I had some fantastic times watching her soaring off from the tops of trees, flashing about in the sky until, after the requisite signal from me, she'd come back to sit on the thick leather gauntlet I wore. It was really quite magical. James also had a wonderful time acting as a kind of gamekeeper for the farmer whose land backed on to our house.

My career at Radio Aire started well. I began working on the night programme. Night-time radio is what I think I do best and it has the added advantage that people listen to the radio at night because they want to. Daytime radio is like wallpaper, it can be on in the background and people don't take much notice of it, but if someone's listening to a radio show at eleven or twelve at night, then chances are, they want to be.

In fact, it was while I was at Radio Aire that I won the first of my industry accolades. I was named Best Personality on Local Radio in 1984. Someone asked me very recently why I don't submit any of my programmes to be considered for the Sony Awards these days. Well, why would I want to? I have absolutely no respect for most of the people who operate radio and judge these so-called honours – I never have had. Most of them don't want people like me on air.

Back in 1984, though, I was persuaded, rather against my will, to attend one of these award ceremonies, seeing as I was one of the nominees. I attended the ceremony with the Radio Aire programme director, a lady called Christa Ackroyd – a woman who I think seems to get mysteriously younger instead of older with each passing year. As I said, I won the award. At the end of the night, Christa, who had clearly enjoyed the evening, somehow managed to drop the bloody thing and it smashed.

That's radio management for you.

During my time at Radio Aire, I encountered one of my later producers, a man called Paul Stead, who now runs his own production company in Yorkshire called Daisybeck Productions. In the years to come, I did my own radio show from studios in Dunstable in Bedfordshire, and Paul produced that programme.

We met for the first time in the mid-eighties. Like a lot of people have done over the years, Paul turned up at Radio Aire one day to ask if he could work for me. He said he loved my programme and he'd like to be connected with it in some way. At that time, he was a chef, and he'd brought some lasagne with him.

'If I give you some of my lasagne, can I work on the show?' he asked.

If I'd known how bad his cooking was, I'd have said no.

It was at this time in my life that I clashed with the law. In the summer of 1987, I was arrested by the Ripon police force. And no, before you ask, it wasn't a publicity stunt.

The day it all happened was a hot, sunny Sunday afternoon. My family and I were all at home, just chilling out. From where I was inside the house, I suddenly heard Melinda shouting at someone. The dogs were going mad too, barking their heads off. My son Peter went outside to see what was happening, and I heard his voice join the mêlée. Never one to stand on the sidelines, I too went out to see what was going on.

We had an uninvited guest in our garden. Some joker in a shellsuit (it *was* the eighties) was ranting on about us having blocked some right of way. This was bollocks: it was a private home. The house may have been situated just off the main road, but that didn't make the property a public thoroughfare. This little man of dubious fashion taste was yelling at my wife, shouting abuse at us all.

Well, I wasn't going to stand for that. Typically forthright, I gave him a piece of my mind. I've always been outspoken and this occasion was certainly no exception. Then, enlisting Peter's help, I picked up this man and together we threw him over the garden gate. With that done, I went inside and phoned the police, to inform them of our trespasser and to let them know what had gone on. I was worried this fool might return a bit later, so I wanted the matter dealt with.

The police said they were too busy to send anyone to look into the situation.

'Okay,' I said, 'but if he comes back, I might kill him.'

That got their attention. A short while later, a tubby policeman turned up to investigate the 'murder threat'. I didn't take it too seriously, but an hour or so after this first officer had made his enquiries, two burly coppers arrived on the scene.

'We want to question you, Mr Whale, and your wife and son,' they said gruffly. 'The three of you will now be interviewed in separate rooms, so that you don't collaborate.'

I didn't think they could possibly be in earnest, so I made what I thought was a harmless joke about us already having got our story straight. It went down like a lead balloon. Before I knew what was happening, I was arrested and taken to Ripon police station for further questioning.

I found myself in a scenario familiar from TV shows like *The Bill*. In a bare room, furnished only with a plain table and uncomfortable chairs, I sat across from the two coppers, the tape recorder between us steadily whirring away, chronicling every moment that passed.

I couldn't resist. Bringing my fist up, I hit myself hard in the chest and gave a powerful accompanying groan (those acting lessons in the seventies really paid off).

'No, please, officers,' I whimpered. 'It's all right, I'll talk.'

The senior officer leant forward to speak into the tape machine. 'The suspect has hit himself in the chest,' he said solemnly.

Oh dear.

I don't know what would have happened if the sergeant hadn't chosen that moment to come in.

'What are you doing with James Whale?' he asked his colleagues.

I should say at this point that he knew me because he was a fan of the radio show. I don't want to give the impression that I was a regular visitor to my local nick.

When the policemen had explained what had happened, the sergeant said: 'Take James home, we know where to find him if we need him.'

I was duly released, and my life of crime was over. Not so for our trespasser, though. We came home one day, not long after that Sunday afternoon, to find our paddock and garden gates wide open. As usual, the traffic was whizzing by. Thankfully, all our animals had been far more interested in tasting grass than freedom, so none had ventured out to what would almost certainly have been a sticky end. There was a note pinned to the open gate. Chillingly, it read: 'Next time, I'll get you all.'

I reported this incident to the police as well, and this time they took a more sensible interest. As it turned out, the trespasser was known to them. He was a mentally disabled individual. There wasn't much the police could do, but luckily 'the shellsuited one' never bothered us again after that.

In the late eighties, I invited Edwina Currie on to my show. At that time, Edwina was a high-profile Tory politician who was a government minister in the Department of Health. She'd become very famous because she'd warned everyone not to eat eggs because they carried strains of salmonella, a controversy over which she eventually resigned. She'd been lambasted in the press for some of her statements, but I got in touch and said I'd like her to come on the show because I liked people who were contentious and had strong opinions, and she fitted the bill.

She wrote back to me and said she'd love to come on the programme the next time she was in Leeds. Coincidentally, she'd just published an article in a newspaper about the benefits of Indian food, particularly tandoori chicken, saying it was one of the healthiest foods you could eat. After seeing that little snippet in the paper, I wrote to her again and said: 'Why don't you come on the programme and I'll take you out for a curry? Because Leeds has got some of the best curry restaurants in the country.'

So, she came on the programme in due course and before we did the show we planned to go out for a curry, which would be good publicity for the programme and for her. She turned up at the radio station to do some photographs and I was waiting outside, ready to escort her to an Indian restaurant for a meal.

'Is that your car?' she asked, pointing at my flash little Japanese sports car.

'Yes,' I told her. 'That's mine.'

'I'll come with you,' she said, jumping into the passenger seat.

Off we went to the restaurant.

What I didn't realize was that she hadn't told any of her little entourage of minders, assistants and sycophants – all those hangers-on who normally follow government ministers around – where she was going. If I didn't know better, I'd have perhaps thought she'd engineered that so she could be alone with me. Regardless of the communication oversight, we arrived safely at the restaurant, where the rest of her entourage found us by and by, all of them rather concerned that I might have popped off somewhere with Edwina.

I wasn't bothered by the fuss. Edwina was a guest on my show. That was my only interest in her and, happily, she was a good guest at the time.

I didn't see her after that until a few years ago, when I was asked to go to a radio conference to talk about what makes a good talk show. Normally, I don't do those kinds of events. I hate that sort of thing where people sit around pontificating about what they do, but the guy who organized it worked at Talk Radio for a time and I liked him, so against my better judgement I agreed to participate.

As it turned out, Edwina Currie was on the panel too. I hadn't seen her for ages, but she, at the time, was doing night-time radio on BBC Radio 5 Live. How, I don't know, because where late-night radio is concerned, she's about as much good as a chocolate fireguard. However, once the panel discussion got going, she proceeded to thank me for encouraging her and for giving her the enthusiasm to work in radio.

This was all news to me. I had no idea that I was responsible for Edwina Currie wanting to be in broadcasting. I can only apologize to the rest of you if it's true.

Luckily, she no longer is. I'd like to be able to take some responsibility for that, too, but unfortunately I can't.

During the discussion, she was spouting on about what makes good radio and I must confess I kept thinking, 'How would this failed politician know what makes good radio?'

She's apparently also written some novels, and I'm sure there are writers everywhere asking the same question about her literary abilities.

Listening to her twittering on was the last straw. I got bored, got up, told them all to fuck off and left. Another example of my trademark charm that endears me to so many people.

It was while I was working at Radio Aire that I received my first real death threat. To be honest, doing the kind of confrontational radio and television shows that I've always done, I've found that it's usually only a matter of time before some nutter somewhere decides that he's had enough of you and you should die. I've therefore always taken threats of this kind with a pinch of salt – frankly, with my image and reputation, they're almost what you might call an occupational hazard.

The source of this particular threat was a guy named Laith Alani. He was a regular caller to the show, who had a tendency to go off into anti-Semitic rants that led to me having to cut him off most of the time. Like all passionate people, he felt strongly about what he rang in about. In fact, he used to turn up at the studio some nights, too. He'd just sit outside on the steps as I was preparing to go home, and I'd chat to him amiably enough on my way out.

That was the curious thing about him. Sitting on the steps of the radio station, he was a polite, erudite and charming young man, and yet when he rang up, he became this racist fiend, barely able to get his point across.

Alani and I talked, both on the air and off it, for months on and off – until one night when I mentioned Ayatollah Khomeini on the show. In the eighties, there was very little of the antagonism between Muslims and Westerners that seems to feature in today's news on a daily basis. That particular evening, I'd decided to talk about Khomeini and how he was preaching hate and violence, encouraging Muslims to be anti-West, and all the other bollocks he spouted. Khomeini really was a dangerous nutcase and his views were straight from the Stone Age. As you can imagine, I wasn't slow in voicing my own opinion of this despotic idiot.

Alani called that night and his sentiments had changed dramatically. The target of his venom was no longer the Jews, it was me. He stopped turning up at the radio station for his little chats. It appeared that I had crossed a line as far as he was concerned.

I was in Nottingham one day when I was approached by two plainclothes policemen. Alani had been arrested, they informed me.

'What for?' I asked.

'Murder,' they told me.

My regular caller had murdered two surgeons in Wakefield, Yorkshire, in cold blood. After Alani's arrest, the police had found what amounted to a death list at his flat. The two surgeons were the first and second names on the list. There are no prizes for guessing who was third. That's right: me.

What especially concerned the police was that Alani was strongly rumoured to have had an accomplice, whom they suspected was responsible for completing the 'removal' of the people on the death list.

From that day on, I had a police escort everywhere I went. They waited for me when I left the radio station at night and one would sit in the car with me as I drove home. Another would then watch the house through the night. This went on for weeks. Ultimately, as far as I know, Alani's accomplice was never caught.

Although this was obviously an extreme example, this kind of reaction *is* the sort a presenter like myself actively seeks. Obviously I don't start off every show with the intention of receiving death threats, but I feel it's necessary to stir up people's feelings, to prompt them into talking about the subjects and matters that they feel most strongly about. If this means people love me, that's great. If they hate me, I can cope with that. At least they're having feelings of some kind about me and the programme, rather than staying uncommitted. Whichever sphere of the entertainment business you happen to work in, the worst reaction you can elicit is indifference.

In my opinion, there are too many people in radio who are frightened of provoking a reaction. They would rather be bland than controversial. I think it's absolutely marvellous that there are new people like Chris Moyles coming through now who understand, in my view, what radio is all about.

I first met Chris when he was a schoolboy and I was a DJ on his local radio station, which was Radio Aire. I remember the first time he came to the station. He came to interview me for his school radio, and that was how we first met. I take pleasure in the fact that Chris says it was listening to and watching me while he was at school in Leeds that inspired him to pursue a career in radio. Chris was about thirteen at the time and his mum used to bring him into the studio. I am so glad he's written about that in his book, *The Gospel According to Chris Moyles*, because it takes away the bad taste that people like Edwina Currie leave when they say I inspired them to go into radio.

For Chris Moyles, I happily accept responsibility. For Edwina Currie, I can only say a heartfelt 'sorry' to you all.

THE STATE OF THE PLANET

I am sick and bloody tired of all this bollocks they're talking about the so-called endangered environment. Global warming, climate change, the melting polar icecaps, carbon emissions ... All this stuff they keep coming up with is just pissing me off.

Climate change is a natural phenomenon and whether you or I drive a four-wheel drive or not isn't going to make a scrap of difference. If there is any effect on the planet caused by what the inhabitants of that planet (i.e. you and I) do, then surely that is natural because we are natural. We live on the bloody planet; what we do while we're on the planet is what naturally shapes the environment.

What we do has a natural purpose. A natural progression.

When the dinosaurs ruled the Earth, the planet wasn't warm because all the tyrannosauruses and triceratops were driving four-by-fours, was it? The Earth was naturally warm. That was the way things were.

Now the Earth is warming up again – not because everyone's going to Tesco in a Jeep, but because the Earth is changing naturally.

Besides, even if everyone is now driving around in Jeeps, then that is simply because it's the natural order. It's a form of evolution. Do you think that cavemen would have gone hunting mammoths on foot if they'd had the option of using a Land Rover? Of course they bloody wouldn't. As a race, we humans adapt and improve our environment and our surroundings to make our lives more comfortable. We don't do so deliberately to destroy our own planet.

Politicians are so bloody thick that they can't seem to grasp the reality of what is happening. Some parts of the globe that are now uninhabitable will become habitable, and vice versa.

What's the problem? There'll be more beach space at the North Pole. That's a good thing as far as I'm concerned. Some parts of Essex will become waterlogged. So what? If it wipes out a few hundred thousand chavs, then who's going to miss them?

Climate change has always happened and it always will. Telling me that recycling my own filth will help just doesn't wash with me.

Every time I open the paper, I am amazed at how gullible people are.

The sea levels have always risen and fallen and that's without blaming it on deodorants. Would politicians rather have a perfect world inhabited by smelly bastards?

Kids at school are forced to believe: 'If my daddy doesn't drive so much, then we'll save the planet.'

Bollocks.

It's not a question of saving the planet; it's a question of adjusting to what the planet has for us.

If there weren't so many books telling us how to stop global warming, then perhaps there'd be a few more trees left in the bloody rainforest.

In fact, those books could be a very good way of solving our lack-of-fuel problem. Don't burn coal or oil. Burn all the bloody books that are scaremongering about global warming. You could also use them for landfill, so that more houses could be built – then people could shelter in them and not risk skin cancer from sunshine that's now bloody dangerous because there's no fucking ozone layer any more.

How's that?

In the final analysis, this problem has been created over hundreds of years. It isn't a problem of our making.

We found the planet like this; we didn't break it.

'I think I should be on television,' I said to Melinda one day.

I was still at Radio Aire. The show was going well and we were happy in our place in Harrogate, so I'm not sure why this ambition suddenly flared. Perhaps it was simply the resurfacing of all those desires I used to have when I worked at Harrods. The need to be recognized, just like all the celebrities I'd seen when I'd worked at that store in London.

'You're better suited to radio,' Melinda told me, but I wasn't convinced. 'Besides, you'll be on the TV when you're thirty-five,' she added.

I wondered if her intuition would be proved correct. All through our life together, she had accurately predicted little things that were going to happen to us and I wondered if she might be right again.

I was thirty-two at the time, however, and I wasn't sure I wanted to wait another three years.

A friend of mine at that time, and today, was Carol Vorderman, who worked next door to the radio station at Yorkshire Television (Radio Aire was located in a bungalow-shaped building situated in a car park, right next to the huge edifice that housed Yorkshire Television, so Carol and I were neighbours as far as work went). Carol used to appear as a guest on my show and she eventually got her own show, too.

'I want to get on TV,' I said to her one day. 'How can I?'

'Go down to London and see my agent,' she advised me.

So I did.

Her agent was called Jackie Evans. 'Why have you left it so long?' Jackie asked me.

'Well, I've been busy,' I answered. 'I've been on the radio and I like doing that – it's just that I feel I should try to make some more money, because I don't want to go into management. That's why I want to do television.'

'What sort of television?' she wanted to know.

'I just want to do what I'm doing on the radio,' I said. 'But do it on TV.' I hadn't really got any idea, to be truthful. I just knew I wanted to be on the box.

'I think I can do something for you,' she said.

I was delighted.

She introduced me to a producer called John Willford, who, I must admit, was a bit off-the-wall, but he was quite a big noise at Yorkshire Television. He was set to produce a new series of programmes for Channel 4, called *The Open College*.

I'd never really done any television before, apart from my work as an extra on *Doctor Who*, *Z Cars* and those other series while I'd been living in London. I'd been interviewed on TV a few times while I was working for Metro Radio in Newcastle, but there's a world of difference between simply being on television and working in it. I'd certainly never fronted a live TV show.

The Open College was envisaged as commercial television's answer to the BBC's *Open University*. John said I'd be an ideal presenter for it – probably because I was smartly dressed and had a pleasing accent. Well, pleasing for that kind of programme anyway.

So, I was given the presenting job, working alongside a succession of females. By the time the series aired, Melinda was proved right: I was on telly, and I was thirty-five.

One day, one of these female presenters and I were doing the show, both of us working to autocue, reading the script that had been written by John Willford, when the autocue on my colleague's camera stopped. I was at the back of the set, doing something I can't remember, when suddenly everything went quiet.

In my earpiece, John was shouting: 'Get on there, for fuck's sake!'

On live TV, my co-presenter had literally run out of things to say. She didn't ad lib. She just stopped talking.

Very scary.

People who've never been on live TV don't understand how frightening it can be. You can rely on the script and if the autocue stops working, if the words just stop, then you can easily be done for. Luckily, my years of experience doing live radio enable me to think on my feet whatever happens. And to be honest, with me being dyslexic, I'm not usually reading the script from the camera anyway (in some ways, a good thing, because you're not supposed to look like you are). Between you and me, I can't see the bloody words, so I'm guessing at them most of the time.

On this occasion, I stepped forward and joked around for a bit, saving both myself and my co-presenter from embarrassment. That was the first time I realized that television could be fun.

The Open College went on for about a year. I don't think it really made any waves in TV. It was appalling. It went out at about one o'clock on a Friday or Monday lunchtime on Channel 4, and I don't think anyone's ever seen it.

If they have, they'd never admit it.

It was live, which was good, set in a 'common room' type of set to make the viewer (and the viewing figures probably were singular, for all I knew) seem as if they were actually at college. After the series finished, I thought my chances of a career in TV had finished, too.

However, about a year later, I got a phone call from a guy called Ian Bolt. I'd never heard of him, but he said: 'James, I'm a big fan of yours. I love your radio show. I want to put it on television.'

'And I'm the Queen of Sheba,' I told him, and hung up.

I thought it was someone winding me up.

It wasn't.

'Have you ever heard of someone called Ian Bolt?' I later asked my agent.

My agent was practically speechless.

'If he's interested in you, that's great,' I was told.

Shit. What had I done?

I'd hung up the phone on a man who wanted to give me my own TV show. A man who was a top producer at Yorkshire Television, a man who produced shows like *3-2-1*, *Through the Keyhole* and various other huge hits. I had to find his number, ring him back and apologize profusely. Luckily, Ian was great about it and it's down to him that *The James Whale Radio Show* on TV started, in 1989.

It was a simple idea: he loved the show on the radio and he wanted to televise it. That was it. Against all odds and despite the wishes of a lot of disgruntled TV executives, who didn't understand what we were doing in those days, we got the show on.

To begin with, it aired only in the Yorkshire and Granada areas, but then, because of the enormous ratings, all over the country. It was weird in a way – I'd travelled from London all those years ago to find employment in my chosen field, and I was now gradually working my way back down the country. Lots of people thought I came from Yorkshire, but it was just that that wonderful county gave me my big break.

For the first year, the TV programme was broadcast live from the radio studio at Radio Aire and it did tremendously well. We used to get 3 million viewers a show, even though it wasn't on until the small hours. It went out on ITV every Friday night from 1 a.m., and the reaction was excellent.

The show went from strength to strength. I couldn't believe the audience response. I'd spent nearly fifteen years of my life working on the radio and I could walk down the street and no one would bat an eyelid. Yet the day after my first TV programme was broadcast, I walked down the street in Harrogate and people looked at me.

After one show!

I really began to appreciate the power of television. I would go to places I'd never been before in my life and people would come up to me and say hello. I visited

Northern Ireland a lot during that time, because the show was particularly popular there, and people treated me as if I was a next-door neighbour. It was wonderful.

Sometimes some of the crew had a few too many drinks and sometimes we went on air without being properly prepared – but that was one of the beauties of the programme. I would guide the viewer through the show as if I was guiding myself. And that's exactly what I was doing. We had no autocue. No script. We were 100 per cent live.

Not every guest appreciated that. Most if not all chat shows, even the live ones, are usually rehearsed before they go on air; even down to the guests knowing which questions they're going to be asked and having ready-made answers prepared, so they don't look bad in front of an audience. I didn't want that. I wanted spontaneity. I wanted danger.

I've found that comedians, in particular, don't like to be caught unawares or forced to work without scripts, in case their reputations for being witty and sharp-minded suffer. I remember being particularly disappointed with Ben Elton – he's everyone's favourite, isn't he? The multimillionaire who still tells jokes about Mrs Thatcher and claims he's a socialist man of the people. He came on the show and he treated it like dirt. He was going on about how politically correct he was. I thought he was a prat. I never had much time for him or his self-important humour, I must admit.

Lots of fantastic guests made appearances. We actually discovered some household names on my TV show. Of course, they'd never admit it now. For example, Steve Coogan was on the programme a lot as a comic, and he got his big break after appearing.

One especially memorable moment was when Jim Bowen (presenter of *Bullseye*) told a dirty story live on air featuring the word 'cunt'. He thought we were in a commercial break. We were actually doing a programme about the origins of swear words and, fortunately, we'd got permission to say 'fuck' and 'cunt' ahead of time. In fact, the episode was called 'The Fuck and Cunt Show'. The idea was to explore the origins of these words – two words that were, and still are, completely taboo as far as live television went. When the episode was conceived, it wasn't with the deliberate intention of shocking people. After all, the programme wasn't transmitted until one o'clock in the morning and anyone who objected could always switch off.

So, we went ahead. We had an Oxford University professor in the studio to explain the roots of these words and to add a little respectability to our arguments. 'Fuck' is quite well known as an old Anglo-Saxon word, but the word 'cunt' is a different matter. The professor explained that the word 'cunt' originated from a street name in the city of London, a street where prostitutes gathered, which was called Great Cunt Street.

The peculiar thing was that even though we had permission to say the words, it still felt really difficult to do so. I said to the floor manager, 'You say them first.' Live on air, I walked up to him and said: 'Now, what are we calling this programme tonight?'

He couldn't say it.

I asked a couple of the cameramen, too, but they couldn't say it either.

It was as if, with permission given, it became more difficult. Had permission not been given, then it might have been easier.

With this newfound freedom, however, Jim Bowen decided he'd tell this very rude story – but he hadn't realized we were still on the air. And let's put it this way: his story *wasn't* an erudite explanation of the etymology of 'cunt'. The incident caused a great deal of fuss and got a large amount of newspaper coverage the following day. Jim was upset because he said his wife had never heard him swear or use the 'c' word in all the years they'd been married.

If she was watching that night, she certainly heard it.

Another guest who created a lot of publicity was Jerry Sadowitz. Jerry is a very funny comedian and magician who was on the show the week after the great entertainer Tommy Cooper died. Cooper had passed away on stage at the London Palladium. That Friday night on my show, Jerry Sadowitz proceeded to do an impression of Tommy, which consisted of him doing a trick and then collapsing, pretending to be dead.

'White rabbit, yellow rabbit,' Jerry Sadowitz grunted in a bad Tommy Cooper voice. 'White rabbit, yellow rabbit … aaarrrggghhh!'

He went down like a stone, clutching his chest. The crew and the other guests were in hysterics.

Not so, some of the viewers.

Within minutes of him completing the impression, our switchboard was jammed with callers howling that Jerry, his act and my show were in bad taste and should be taken off the air. We had more than four hundred calls of complaint from the Tommy Cooper Appreciation Society alone.

But that's the kind of thing you have to expect on live TV. The trick is learning how to deal with situations like that.

When Wayne Hussey, then the lead singer with the band The Mission, showed up drunk on the show, I threw him out live on the air. Lemmy, the lead singer of rock band Motörhead, did the same thing and suffered the same fate.

You deal with the situation and that's how I dealt with it. If people are tuning in to your TV show, they don't want to sit watching some drunken slurring idiot spoiling things. To me, that smacks of unprofessionalism and that's something I hate. As a presenter, I have a duty to my viewers and listeners to give them something worthwhile to watch or listen to, and seeing some pissed-up rock star lurching about or slumped in his seat isn't most people's idea of entertainment.

Whether seeing me storm off my own show counts as entertainment I don't know, but towards the end of the first series of *The James Whale Radio Show*, that was precisely what I did.

It was a normal Friday night. The show was going to air. Everything was ready. The guests, among them Sinitta, the singer, were on standby. The floor manager counted me in and *The James Whale Radio Show* took to the air on Yorkshire Television in its usual slot.

I was having technical problems from the beginning. My earpiece was playing up; I couldn't hear the director properly through it. It wasn't a good start. I was becoming more agitated by the minute.

The floor manager tried to placate me. I was given a new earpiece (all this in full view of the cameras, as we were live) and the show continued.

So too did the problems. Now the new earpiece was playing up. I still couldn't hear the director through it and although he was communicating with the floor manager as well, I was struggling. I was also becoming angrier. Why the hell couldn't they get these simple problems fixed?

We got to the second break and still there was no improvement. That was it. The last straw. Just after the second break, I threw a wobbler of monumental proportions.

'I've never worked on anything so amateurish,' I shouted, live on the air. I then ripped my earpiece out, got to my feet and simply walked out of the studio.

The floor manager and all but one of the cameramen went crazy. I was walking out in the middle of a live show. This just wasn't done.

I stormed out. Fuming with anger, I walked off the set and towards the rear entrance of the studios, with one cameraman still following me as I headed across the car park to my car, got in and roared off. That was it. Done. Finished. I'd walked out of my own show.

The following day, the newspapers were full of it.

I was missing for a week. Nina Myskow, the television critic and one of the good guys, presented the show the following Friday.

Me? I was in Chicago, with an American policeman friend called Mike. He'd rung the show once and told me that if I was ever in Chicago, I should look him up, that he'd take me around the city in his police car and let me see what went on.

So, for a week, while almost everyone at Yorkshire TV was wondering what the hell had happened, and as the national newspapers provided me with the kind of publicity I wanted for the show, I spent my time riding around in a Chicago squad car seeing the darker side of that city.

Mike was a wonderful host. Together, we patrolled some of the more menacing and dangerous areas of Chicago, with him as my guide and bodyguard. We were walking down Rush Street at one point, the home of so many blues clubs, when Mike suddenly grabbed a black man and slammed him down over the bonnet of a car.

'What are you doing?' I asked in surprise.

'We know he's killed a couple of people, but we can't prove it,' Mike said, calmly. 'We're hassling him. Trying to provoke him into doing something so we can arrest him.'

The way the police acted there was so different to how our own law-enforcement people behave, it was like being on another planet.

Another night Mike, Graham Pollard (the director of my TV show, who was filming our trip for the programme) and I were out in Mike's car, driving around downtown, when a woman pulled out in front of us. As she'd almost driven into us, Mike hit his hooter by way of a warning. The woman jumped out of her car and – as the Americans are fond of saying – 'flipped him the bird'. She stuck her middle finger up at him.

Mike was out of his own car in seconds.

'Stay here,' he told Graham and me.

We did as we were told and watched Mike with this woman who, by now, was shouting madly at him. Mike was in plain clothes at the time so she had no way of knowing he was a policeman.

'What the hell do you think you're doing?' she yelled, even though she had been the one in the wrong. 'If there was a policeman around, I'd report you,' she went on.

Mike smiled and produced his badge. 'There is a policeman around,' he said. 'You're the one who's in trouble.'

In the car, Graham and I were laughing as we watched. It was just one of many instances that week when we saw what it was like to be a Chicago policeman.

One of the most interesting places Mike took us to was the Biograph Theatre, the cinema outside which John Dillinger was shot in 1933. Dillinger was public enemy number one at that time (it was his second time, actually; I think I'm right in saying he was one of the few people ever to be accorded that dubious accolade twice). Dillinger, his girlfriend, and a woman called Anna Sage (more popularly known as the Lady in Red, because of her penchant for wearing that colour) had gone to the cinema that evening to watch a gangster film called *Manhattan Melodrama*. What Dillinger didn't know was that Sage had tipped off the FBI with his whereabouts. When he emerged from the Biograph later that night, he was shot and killed by the FBI's leading agent, a man called Melvin Purvis. So, the most famous gangster in America was betrayed by a bloody woman. Typical.

Mike showed us lots of places like that, and other locations that had been significant during the Prohibition era and the reign of Al Capone. Basically, I had a week's holiday – then I came back and continued presenting the show once more.

To this day, people who saw me walk out on my show have wondered why the series didn't fold that very Friday night. The answer is simple: the whole thing was a set-up. I never had technical problems with my earpiece. I never threw a spontaneous wobbler over bad equipment. It was all planned. Designed to get even more publicity for the show – and it worked like a charm. It was a fantastic publicity stunt.

In fact, it was originally meant to be a stunt on behalf of the army. They'd contacted the show and asked if they could kidnap and then 'rescue' me live on the air in order to get some publicity for themselves. Logistically, this wasn't possible. Not wanting to pass up the opportunity of some PR for the show, I instead staged what looked like a genuine walkout from my own programme.

It was planned under tight security. From the crew, only Graham (the director), the producer and one of the cameramen were in on it. The latter's involvement explains why the camera managed to follow me through the building and into the car park beyond without missing a shot. Sinitta, my guest that night, was also in the know: she smoothly took over presenting the show after I'd stormed out. Even now, it amazes me that no one in the industry who saw that programme suspected that it was a carefully contrived hoax. But the truth is, they were set up and it worked like a dream. The ratings for the next show were even higher. That was the kind of thing you could do with a show like ours.

No one has ever managed to do a programme like mine since. Chris Evans must have watched it and been influenced by it and he tried to do a very similar thing with his show *TFI Friday*, but with lots of money thrown at him. The way we used to do it was on a shoestring budget and that was the charm of it.

Some of you reading this might think that working in TV sounds glamorous – trips to Chicago, interacting with the nation's top performers, singers and comedians. It's a common falsehood that all TV is glamorous. Let me tell you: it really isn't. A story from around this time is a good example of that fact.

As you may know, we used to cover some fairly risqué subjects on the show. One Friday, we were doing an episode about porn stars. So, we had one on the programme – a very successful young lady who made her not inconsiderable living working as an actress in porn movies.

Our usual routine after the programme was that we – the whole crew and any guests – would go to the bar at Yorkshire TV. On this night, the porn star decided that she'd join me, the producer, the director and a couple of the cameramen for a few drinks. We closed up the radio studio, where we'd been filming, and were already walking to the Yorkshire TV building when she said: 'I've got to have a pee. I must have a pee.'

'The radio studio's all locked up,' Ian Bolt, the producer, told her. 'We'll be inside Yorkshire TV studios in five minutes. You'll be able to go to the toilet then.'

'I can't wait, I can't wait!' she shrieked.

She then proceeded to get us all to stand around her in a circle, facing outwards of course, while she squatted down over a manhole cover and had a pee in the car park of Radio Aire.

Ah, the glamour of television.

For some reason, the executives at Yorkshire TV decided to drag their heels when re-commissioning my show for a new series so, pissed off at their indecision, I went off and found some willing people at London Weekend Television who wanted me.

In truth, I felt fortunate that they did. Not everyone who works in TV goes on to have a glittering career. It's a common misconception that everyone on TV is constantly working in the medium; another is that everyone on TV is rich. Neither is true. Of course, many people in television are obscenely overpaid when you look at their talent in ratio to their wage packet, but, unfortunately, that's just the way it is.

I did a programme for LWT at the start of the nineties called *Dial Midnight*. It went out live from their London studios. It was a local London show broadcast just in the capital. The director and producer was a guy called Paul Lewis (not the same Paul Lewis who worked at Metro back in the seventies). I was thrust on to him while they were waiting for a slot to become vacant for my next eponymous show.

On *Dial Midnight*, I used to sit on a red sofa with two girls – Samantha Norman, the daughter of TV film critic Barry Norman, and Anastasia Cook. They were both Sloane Ranger-type girls, frightfully well spoken and very posh. They didn't like me at all. Samantha used to say to me: 'It's so nice to have a bit of rough on the show, darling.' I did two series of *Dial Midnight*, and then I teamed up with producer Mike Mansfield for a couple of series of *Whale On* (on which more later), a pre-recorded show broadcast in my favourite Friday night slot.

During the time I was doing my own TV show, I did lots of other television as well. Among the shows I fronted was an audience discussion programme called *Central Weekend*, which was filmed in Birmingham at the studios of Central Television. It went out live on a Friday night, at 10.30 p.m., and ran for ninety minutes, during which time there'd be three different debates, on everything from issues that were at the forefront of the news at the time, to whether or not drugs were a good thing, to whether pets were psychic. The usual kind of fodder for that sort of programme. Four guests, two supporting the argument and two opposing it, would sit on the stage and give their viewpoints, and then the audience would weigh in with their opinions. The show sometimes degenerated into a shouting match, but that kind of bear-pit mentality was what the producers wanted and it contained the element of uncertainty so necessary to successful live television.

I co-presented the show with a female presenter and another male presenter. My colleagues would vary from programme to programme. One of the women with whom I worked was Kay Adams, who presented *Loose Women*. One of my male colleagues was a chap called Nicky Campbell. I think he's a plonker. As far as I can see, he's obsessed with the way he looks and how marvellous he is.

One night, he and I had gone out for a bite to eat after rehearsals for the show. We were traversing a zebra crossing when a car almost didn't stop. Campbell was absolutely beside himself. Not, as you might expect, because of the fact that we'd both almost been hit by a bloody car, but because he wanted to know whether it would have been him or me who'd have made the headlines in the newspapers the following day. That about sums him up as far as I'm concerned.

As you probably know, he now works in radio – but then again, who doesn't these days? I think his biggest problem with radio must be that no one can see him while he's working.

Central Weekend threw up the requisite amount of memorable moments and also objectionable guests. One in particular that I remember was an obnoxious little shit who was, at the time, probably the most odious person I'd ever interviewed. He was a stage hypnotist who'd come to the attention of the show's researchers because of his own vile and disgusting show, in which he hypnotized people into having sex with each other, imagining they were about to shit themselves, and other such tasteful acts. He was on the segment of the show that I was introducing. We showed some tape of him hypnotizing a woman into thinking that she'd lost her breasts. She was seen looking horrified, fumbling under her chair and in her handbag for them, and this little shit on the stage in the *Central Weekend* studio started laughing.

'You find that funny, do you?' I asked him.

He immediately became very aggressive and I remember having to restrain him, sitting on him to keep him in his seat, until security arrived to eject him.

I guess I should count myself lucky he didn't try to hypnotize me.

People have asked me over the years who the most annoying, objectionable or hateful person I've ever interviewed is, but to be honest, I couldn't say that one name springs to mind above all others. I always go into a show, whether on TV or radio, with an open mind, and if the person I'm interviewing puts their viewpoint across in a civilized and erudite manner, then that's fine.

If I do happen to find someone particularly vile, I don't tend to react to that aggressively, the way some interviewers do. Believe it or not, it actually takes a lot to annoy me. Self-important people tend to irritate me more than most. So, a big hello to Nicky Campbell, Vanessa Feltz and any alternative comedians reading this.

My eponymous TV shows, such as *The James Whale Radio Show* and *Whale On*, were basically always the same sort of thing, they just went out under different titles. The programmes were never as anarchic at LWT as they had been at Yorkshire, though. The main reason for this was that, because of financial considerations, *Whale On* couldn't go out live. It was recorded 'as live', but there's a huge difference to a real live programme. The material doesn't get edited, but you're always aware that you've got that safety net if something goes horribly wrong; a safety net you just don't have on a live show.

For *Whale On*, we used to record two shows back to back on a Monday evening, in a studio just off Carnaby Street in London, and we had some good guests and some good times. That was, financially, the only way we could do it. At that time, TV companies were cutting back on their budgets, and it was becoming increasingly difficult to get audiences to come out as well.

Screaming Lord Sutch, of the Official Monster Raving Loony Party, appeared on one of the programmes. He actually performed live, something he rarely did in those days. He did a set with his band that culminated in his top hat catching fire: a gimmick that, for some unknown reason, was never popular with TV executives. Perhaps it was too spontaneous for them. Screaming Lord Sutch was a great guy – he even had a gift for me that night. He'd brought back from America a jacket that he'd picked out especially for me. It was covered in embroidered whales.

Working on *Whale On* was like being part of a big family, perhaps because Mike Mansfield was a good mate of mine as well as being a talented producer. Nevertheless, I really missed the live shows. I wanted the danger and uncertainty.

Once again, my restlessness began to gnaw away at me. Though I was enjoying my time on television, I felt there were more things to be done in radio. I wanted a new challenge on the airwaves.

I'd been doing some radio during this time, of course, though by now I'd left Radio Aire. It was the early nineties and I'd been doing a weekend show on LBC for two years. These broadcasts were based at their Hammersmith studios, some of the best I've ever worked in.

On one of these shows I replaced the late George Best. He did not like me at all. George was most upset that they'd stopped sport on LBC, and he was particularly rude to me when I joined the station. It wasn't even his show that I took over; he was just one of many contributors. LBC felt they'd attract a bigger audience with a show like mine, and they were subsequently proved right. Mr Best, however, was not convinced.

I must say that I think, in his latter days, he was rather a sad individual, held in awe by those who insisted on living in the past. Namely, *his* past. Yes, he was a wonderful footballer when he played, but let's be honest, the guy was a part-time footballer and a full-time drunk. I think he should have received far more criticism for the way he behaved towards the end of his life, though that's just my humble opinion.

In 1990, I turned thirty-nine. It was the last birthday I celebrated. I don't celebrate my birthdays any more. What's the point? When you get to a certain age, a birthday is just another day. A reminder of how old you're getting. Sod that.

In spite of that incipient viewpoint, my thirty-ninth birthday was a happy event. Melinda and I were living in Yorkshire, I was getting strong ratings for my TV and radio shows, pursuing my chosen career. Life was good. We were living next door to American service people, who were great neighbours, so I decided to have a huge barbecue to celebrate the big day. People from the TV show came, lots of friends came. One of those who turned up was Eamonn Holmes, who wasn't quite as well known back then as he is today.

Poor old Eamonn. He'd just bought himself a secondhand Jaguar XJ6, but he arrived looking very glum.

'What's wrong?' I asked.

'I bought this car and my wife says we can't afford it,' he told me. 'We had a big argument.'

He cheered up as the barbecue progressed. The Americans from next door filled up the dustbin with ice and shoved beer into it. I'd never seen anyone do that before. I got chatting to Eamonn, who hadn't got much work at the time. In fact, I put him in for a couple of jobs at Yorkshire Television, quiz shows that he hosted and which did remarkably well. Of course, he's since become a TV superstar.

I didn't see him for a long time when he did *GMTV*. We were at different times of the day in different parts of the world, but, recently, we've got back in touch as we've been doing newspaper reviews together on Sky

TV. It's been nice to get to know him again – he's a great guy.

I first met him when he was presenting a programme called *Open Air* on BBC TV, nearly twenty years ago. I'd been invited on as a guest to spout off, as I do occasionally, and we became pals.

I always wanted to do a TV show with Eamonn called *The Rough and the Smooth*. Obviously, I'd be the smooth. Regrettably, it never happened.

I used to drive a nippy little Japanese sports car when we first met.

'Why don't you get a Mercedes?' Eamonn asked me.

'I can't afford a Mercedes,' I protested.

However, eventually I did swap my little sports car for a Mercedes saloon – which actually cost less – and I've loved Mercedes ever since. They can have thousands of miles on the clock and yet still feel as if they're brand new when you're driving them. They're made to last; something that doesn't happen very much in life today. I'll always thank Eamonn for converting me.

A year or so after that birthday barbecue, I was driving around the Yorkshire Dales with Melinda one day. We were just listening to the radio, when we suddenly picked up a station called Atlantic 252. It was a long-wave radio station, playing all the kinds of music I liked and broadcasting from Dublin.

I got in touch with my agent. 'Listen,' I said. 'I'd like to do some more radio. See if you can get me on Atlantic 252.'

I ended up doing a Sunday morning breakfast show on there for a time. It nearly killed me.

I used to fly to Dublin every Saturday night. I'd get picked up from the airport by an allotted driver and taken to the digs: a pub next to the radio station. The station itself was in County Meath, about twenty-five miles outside Dublin. Driving there with this guy was the most horrific experience – he never seemed to look where he was going – so I was always relieved when we arrived in one piece. I'd go and have a pint of Guinness and a chat with the people in the pub, and then I'd go to bed, ready to be up at six the next morning. I'd do the show, bright and early, the driver would then take me back to the airport in Dublin, and I'd fly home.

Melinda, quite rightly, thought that it was something that couldn't go on for too long, and after six months, I packed it in. I did enjoy it, though, and it further fuelled my desire to get back into radio full-time. So when I heard, a couple of years later in 1994, that a new talk-radio station was being discussed, to launch on air in February 1995, I was really excited. This was the opportunity I'd been waiting for.

At the time the idea for Talk Radio was first mooted, I was still doing my weekly television show with Mike Mansfield, *Whale On*. I also had my weekend radio show on LBC and a Sunday morning show for BBC Radio London. Obviously, I didn't do them all at the same time. Nonetheless, lots of people knew of my work both on TV and radio.

Confident of my own abilities and the fact that I'd served my apprenticeship on all my other radio shows over the past two decades, I got myself a meeting with the people who were running Talk Radio. Within a couple of days, I went to meet the management – for what I thought would be a relatively routine interview. I anticipated that with my years of experience on the radio they'd be delighted to have me. However, as had been the case so many times before with clueless people running radio stations, they simply had no fucking idea what they were doing.

The guy I had the interview with said, 'Well, James, I'm told you've done some radio, but I'm not aware of your radio work.'

Basically, everybody in radio knew that I'd worked in the business since the early seventies. Everybody, it seemed, except this guy, who'd got a job on a national radio station.

He continued, 'We're trying to stay away from TV celebrities who want to get on radio. I really am loath to take on a TV personality who may not know what radio is all about.'

Well, that was a red rag to a bull. I got up, preparing to leave. 'Look, pillock face,' I snapped. 'You'll last six months. You will ruin this radio station and when you're going out the door, I'll be coming in.'

With that show-stopping exit line, I walked out.

What did I do next? I went back to Mike Mansfield and did another series of *Whale On*. If I was honest, though, my heart was set on getting back into radio again. Happily, as I'd suspected, I didn't have to wait too long. In what seemed like no time, the whole Talk Radio enterprise went tits up. They made a complete cock-up of the station. They hired a lot of the wrong people; they scheduled a lot of the wrong programming. Talk Radio was losing a million pounds a month because they couldn't get the audience.

As you'd expect with any such balls-up in your own industry, new bosses were duly appointed. The first I knew about it was when I got a phone call from Jason Bryant. I'd known Jason for a while and he'd been taken on to bring it all together. The first thing he did was get rid of most of the idiots who'd been working there. The next thing he did was ring me.

'I'd love to do a show, but I can't commit to very much at the moment,' I told him – truthfully, as I was still doing *Whale On* at the time.

'What about one Saturday night, something like that?' he enquired.

Jeremy Beadle had been doing that slot previously, but didn't want to carry on.

Jason persisted and, eventually, I agreed to sign up with Talk Radio in 1996. As Jason had promised, I just did one night a week to start with, but that one night was gradually extended once I had more free time and could commit to more hours on air.

Not long after I'd started there, I bumped into one of the guys I'd met at the first interview. We were in the lift together. I was coming in. He was on his way out. He just looked at me and said: 'Don't say anything.'

My prophecy, it seemed, had come true.

'You've only got yourself to blame,' I told him.

God, what a patronizing cunt I can be at times.

As anyone in the entertainment business will tell you, when you reach a certain level of public awareness (I won't use the word 'fame' because I hate it), you become of interest to newspapers. The things you do and say suddenly seem important to journalists and editors. It's the price you have to pay for doing the job you do.

Some people don't seem willing to pay that price. Frankly, all these so-called celebrities who constantly bleat on about not having any privacy should shut up and appreciate the kind of lifestyle they enjoy. It really gets my goat, these stars who are always complaining about being photographed coming out of Langan's or The Ivy. There's a simple solution in my opinion: don't eat there. There are thousands of restaurants in London. If you don't want to be photographed, then don't eat at places where you know the paparazzi are going to be. It isn't rocket science.

My own opinion of the paparazzi, newspapers and journalists, however, is somewhat ambivalent. I realize that these people have jobs to do, but I just wish that sometimes they would stop to think of the hurt they cause – not to the people they are writing about, but to those close to them. I say this because, not having been the best behaved person in the world, sometimes Melinda has suffered because of things I've done. I appreciate, though, that I can blame the papers for publishing articles about me, but when those articles are true, obviously the only person who is ultimately to blame for any hurt is me. In 1997, I was rudely awakened to that fact, when a woman sold a story about me to the tabloid press, and the Sunday papers had a field day writing about me and my supposed promiscuous lifestyle.

Now, I'll be the first to admit, I have dallied from time to time over the years – because opportunities have arisen. But I'm a man. I offer that not as mitigation, but as an explanation. Men think with their dicks more than their heads. Men view casual sex in a completely different way to most women. It just seems to be easier for men to stray, because they don't have the emotional needs that women have. That's why men go to lap-dancing clubs. That's why they have men's nights out.

There are women, of course, who are able to approach sex with the same dispassionate approach as men, but frankly they're thinner on the ground. Women usually need the security of a loving relationship before they can hurl themselves into bed with someone. Men don't. Women invariably require someone to care emotionally about them before they can embark on some random roll in the hay. Men don't.

These dalliances that I had occasionally happened because I didn't realize I was upsetting Melinda. Mainly because I didn't think she would ever find out about them. What the eye doesn't see, the heart doesn't grieve over, as the old saying goes.

In fact, one thing I can be vaguely proud of is that I never said to any of my casual acquaintances, 'My wife doesn't understand me. I don't love her. Our marriage is breaking up.' I used none of the usual clichés that men use with their bits on the side.

I know this doesn't make my behaviour any more acceptable, but that's what happened. I'm not going to try to hide behind excuses. I'm just telling you the truth.

If I had to give one specific reason why these indiscretions occurred, I'd say it was because I was making up for lost time. I married Melinda when I was nineteen and I probably felt that I was missing out on all those other women out there. I'd only just started going out with girls, for heaven's sake, when James came along. I'd just discovered the opposite sex ... and then there I was married to the same woman for the rest of my life. A friend of mine went through exactly the same experience with his wife.

Men and women who marry early, particularly those who go on to have children when they're young, invariably feel as if they've missed out on something. The truth is they haven't, but something inside them keeps convincing them that they would have had more partners if they'd stayed single longer. Probably a fallacy, but they cling to that thought as an excuse for their infidelities.

There may be some of you reading this now who are sitting in judgement. That's fine if you are, but I'll say this to you: I don't think there is one man out there (or woman, too), who, given the right circumstances and opportunity, wouldn't cheat on their other half. If there was no chance in the world of being caught, found out or exposed, I am willing to bet that 99.9 per

Above: Me with my grandfather, Vivien, in 1951, shortly after I'd been born.

Below: Big brother: me with my baby brother Keith.

Right: No place like home: Mum and Dad behind the bar of The Harrison Arms in the late sixties.

Family man: with my three-month-old son, James, in 1970 (*above*); with both my sons, James and Peter, in Newcastle in the late seventies (*left*); as a proud granddad with Peter's son from his second marriage, Oscar, on holiday in Monte Carlo (*below*).

Left: The rudest man on British radio?: the *Sunday People* announced its verdict using this specially staged picture.

Below: Recovering after breaking a world record: kissing more women in eight hours than anyone else.

CERTIFICATE

SONY
RADIO
AWARDS
1987

SONY.

SONY
RADIO
AWARDS
1988

CERTIFICATE

Left: Two of my Sony Awards: these I won in consecutive years for Local DJ of the Year.

Left: With my loyal producer, Mike Mansfield, and a drag queen, during rehearsals.

Right: With Cookie, my glamorous assistant on the TV show.

Below: I've met some colourful characters over the years – here I am with Screaming Lord Sutch of the Official Monster Raving Loony Party.

On the run: at the airport checking out the press reports of my walkout stunt on *The James Whale Radio Show*.

With my getaway buddy, Sergeant Michael Blackburn, in Chicago, USA.

Left: Receiving the award for Spectacle Wearer of the Year. The annual event was my idea.

Above: With Pauline Edwards MBE, the British archery champion.

Left: At the launch of my kidney cancer charity in 2006, with actor Billy Murray, club owner Peter Stringfellow and Melinda.

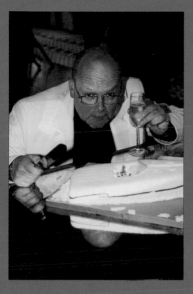

At my fiftieth birthday party, shortly after beating cancer.

With Melinda and *Daily Mail* writer David Wigg at the bash.

On holiday in Prague with (*l-r*) the *Blade II* make-up artist, Luke Goss, Luke's wife Shirley, Luke's manager and Melinda.

Left: With my son Peter and Melinda in our restaurant in Harrogate.

Below: As a kid, I always wanted to be a cowboy. This is the closest I've come, on a photo shoot in 2006.

Below: Me and Melinda with our dog, Frisby. He's more trouble than he looks.

cent of all human beings would indulge in a little indiscretion if the opportunity arose. If you say you wouldn't, then you're lying to yourself. And that includes the journalists who wrote all those stories about me.

What's that other saying about people living in glass houses not throwing stones? It seems to me that some journalists find that one rather easy to ignore. Investigate most reporters, male and female, and you'll quickly find the kind of seething hypocrisy that they claim to be so eager to expose.

What I am truly sorry for is the pain my indiscretions caused to those I love; that includes my mother, who, I later discovered, kept all the cuttings of my well-publicized mistakes. I didn't have to face up to all this hurt until I was plastered over the front of the Sunday papers.

Even now, the only reason I can imagine I made the front pages is because it was what the press call a 'slow news' weekend. In other words, fuck all else was going on and they had nothing else to write about, so they wrote about me. In any case, I certainly didn't realize, until this particular story appeared in the papers, in February 1997, that I was well known enough or of sufficient interest to be on the front page of the *News of the World* or the *Mirror* or the *People*.

Those headlines forced me to confront what I'd done. It isn't a nice thing to have to face up to the fact that you're a complete bastard. That's how I think of myself now for what I did to Melinda.

At the time when it was actually going on, I tried to handle it in my own way. I tried to dismiss the indiscretions in my own mind. But there's something about seeing it all in black-and-white newsprint that makes it impossible to ignore.

Basically, the story was this. One particular female fan phoned me on the show and wrote to me, expressing her appreciation of what I did. For some reason, late-night radio DJs and presenters have a sort of sexy image about them that is quite attractive to certain kinds of listener. This has always been the case and no doubt it always will be. I don't know why it should be. To this day, it baffles me. Certainly in my case it does. However, I made the most basic mistake of anyone in my position when I heard from this woman. I agreed to meet her.

I had the feeling that what I was doing was stupid. Anyone who's been in the same position will understand what I mean, because this doesn't just apply to people in the entertainment business. Everyone's been tempted in their lives, I'm sure. It's just that being in the public eye makes you that little bit more appealing, so there are even more temptations to resist.

Looking back on what happened, I can't believe I went through with it. I knew what I was doing wasn't right, and yet I still did it. In my mind, I was never doing it because I didn't love Melinda. I was doing it because I could. Pure and simple.

When this woman made her approach, I was amazed. I had never considered that I was well known. I worked late at night. It wasn't as if I had a prime-time TV show that was going out all over the country.

Whatever the case, I met this woman and, after the inevitable had happened, she sold her story to the tabloid press.

One of those papers then arranged for a man to

follow me around, photographing me. I knew nothing about this. I hadn't got a clue I was being followed. I didn't think that my life would be of any interest to anyone, let alone major national newspapers.

Of course, I was wrong.

This woman rang me at the radio station one morning. 'When are we going out?' she wanted to know.

For some reason, I was sure then that she was recording the conversation and trying to elicit some incriminating response from me.

I don't know how much she eventually sold her story for, but I haven't had so much press coverage in my entire life. It was insane.

When the story broke, Melinda and I sat down and talked. I didn't want her to be seen as the helpless little lady who stuck by her man, even though I desperately didn't want to lose her. As it turned out, Melinda's public image was the least of her worries. I had had no idea how hurt, upset and completely destroyed Melinda would be on learning of my indiscretion.

She and I stayed up all night talking about what had happened. There weren't really any shouting matches, and that in itself was quite disconcerting. I was expecting a furious verbal battle, but Melinda was remarkably calm. She decided that she'd come to Manchester with me the next day, where I was doing a live outside broadcast, and I didn't blame her. In all honesty, she could hardly function after what she'd read in the papers. She barely knew what day it was.

It sounds ridiculous, but I didn't realize until that time how much she loved me. I know it's pathetic that it took my own infidelity to confirm this, but that's just the way it was. I also didn't realize how much I loved her, how much my life was intertwined with Melinda's. We were one person. I mean, we had different interests, obviously. I think a relationship where the husband and wife share absolutely the same views and interests is boring. The world thrives on difference and that's also true in a marriage or any long-term relationship. Somehow, Melinda and I struck just the right balance and I'm ashamed it took me so long to realize it. In fact, when I discovered a few years later that I had got cancer, a part of me thought: 'Good. I deserve it. I deserve to be punished.'

The day after the story broke, I was suddenly faced with a barrage of people outside my house, all ringing me up, asking for statements and trying to photograph me. I didn't know how to cope with it because I'd never been in that position before. You could say that everyone in the entertainment business wants to be well known, but not in that way. No one wants newspapermen following them twenty-four hours a day.

If it hadn't been for Max Clifford, the PR guru (as the papers call him), guiding us through the press interest, I don't know what we would have done. Melinda and I certainly didn't know how to handle this unexpected and unwanted attention. I will be eternally grateful to Max for the way he steered us through the minefield of questions and intrusions.

Inevitably, not only were the journalists following me, they were also following Melinda. One day, soon after this absurd blanket coverage commenced, she was carving some meat and she cut her finger quite badly. Whether she hadn't been concentrating because of what was going on I don't know, but the cut was bad enough that she had to seek medical attention. Her mum drove her to the Accident and Emergency department at Harrogate Hospital. That fact appeared in the newspapers, but the accompanying story maintained that she'd had to go to hospital because she'd attacked me. Journalists had obviously followed her to A&E, put two and two together and come up with five.

After that fallacious story appeared, the *Sunday Mirror* agreed to print Melinda's side of the story – which was actually better than a retraction.

Nevertheless, there's no getting away from it: it was a very, very upsetting time. It upset Melinda and it upset my kids. I've never really looked on myself as a good husband or a good father. All this really seemed to cement that belief.

I know that society's bottom line is that once you're married, you don't mess around, but that isn't the reality for anyone, I don't think. Temptation comes in many forms and everyone is susceptible to temptation, no matter what they may say. And, in my case, no matter what they look like.

To this day, I don't like confronting this subject. I find it very difficult to express these thoughts. I was prepared to blank it out of my mind completely. Men are very good at that: we do things, then pretend they never happened.

It may sound crazy, but had some of these things *not* happened, I honestly don't think that I'd have the close relationship with Melinda that I do today. We fight a lot and we argue a lot, but I couldn't live without her. She's a wonderful woman and she's a tough woman – not the subservient little wife she might appear to be. Trust me, to deal with a situation like that you need more strength than you do in a normal relationship. Going through married life without any ups and downs is easy. Having to work at a relationship takes real strength and courage, and Melinda has those qualities in spades.

What I do want to make clear is that Melinda has never forgiven me, not to this day, and I'm happy in that knowledge. What I did was appalling and I don't feel that I deserve her forgiveness. She loves me, but part of me she doesn't like, and I appreciate that. I know that when I did what I did, I killed the trust she had for me, and I also know that I'll never live long enough to regain that trust. It's a price I accept I have to pay.

The woman who sold her story about me did the same thing a few months later with a judge. She'd been working in the law courts and she accused one of the judges of trying to seduce her.

There are young women out there who seem to make their living doing that kind of thing. There have been a number in the newspapers recently who've made a career out of selling stories about footballers they've slept with. They seem to move from one player to the next, making a few bob along the way from telling all to the papers. It's a sordid little industry, but it goes on and it will continue to as long as people want to read these revelations.

And as long as there are foolish people like me to write about.

LET'S PAUSE HERE FOR A MOMENT ...

IMMIGRATION FOR THE NATION

I'm an endangered species. I'm a white, middle-class man. It isn't trendy to be white, middle class and proud of it. There's not many of us about.

Over the years, we have allowed people to come to this country and take it over.

As simple as that.

At the moment, our society seems to be obsessed with racism, so my views on all this will probably make some ignorant people accuse me of being racist. I'm sure I'm not racist. In fact, I know I'm not racist because for me the issue surrounding immigration isn't about the colour of your skin, it's about how much you contribute to society. I believe that this country has handed far too much to people who come to this place and don't give anything in return. In general, British people are happy to open their arms and invite anyone from any corner of the world. That's one of the great things about this nation. But as far as I'm concerned, if you come to this country, then you *must* contribute to British life.

What we should have done all those years ago was to say that anyone who wants to come here, who wants to become British, who wants to contribute to society, is welcome. If people seeking asylum want to come here, then fine – as long as they can prove they're here because they chose this country and not just because they think they're going to get an easy ride. They shouldn't come to take the piss out of our welfare services that are staffed, as far as I can see, by a load of misguided do-gooders. (The British people who really need help never seem to get it. And let's be clear: when I say British, it could be someone with black skin, brown skin or yellow skin. If they were born here, they're British.)

However, I say categorically that I'm not interested in accommodating those immigrants who want to come to this country and form little areas that are like countries of their own. I don't care what colour they are or where they come from or what religion they are. In fact, if they have no religion at all that would be even better, because organized religion is a bad thing. It was created by man, not God, and it's a divisive thing designed to keep people apart.

I say, stop the power of the church. Kick the bishops out of the House of Lords. Lock up any mad mullah who preaches hate against this country, which has given him and his family somewhere to live. Stop allowing the human-rights laws to be twisted.

We should get rid of religious schools. Fancy sending your kids to a school to be indoctrinated in something that you yourself believe in! People should allow their children to develop in their own way. Permit kids to come to their own conclusions using their own arguments and beliefs.

I believe in God, or in some kind of divine creator, because everything seems to have a place in the grand scheme of things. Everything seems to have a purpose.

What I don't believe is that that creator is also the creator of the Bible or the Koran or any other book. Many do, I realize that and I respect it, but don't try to force your ideas on me.

I say the same to those who come to this country and don't integrate: don't try to force your views on me. If you want to come and live here, then come by all means, but be a contributor to the wealth of the nation. Be a part of the nation. Britain's failure to insist on this has left us in a position where there's strife between different cultures.

We have got to get rid of the religious divisiveness in this country. I find it hilarious that the only thing that unites religions is their hatred of homosexuals. Of all the important matters in the world today, the only thing that every religion is united about is which hole you stick your dick in. That just about says it all.

Seriously, though, as far as I'm concerned, there are certain things in the modern-day culture of this country that are not acceptable; certain things that are happening because some people refuse to be a part of British life. For example, it isn't acceptable for people to put their religion before the law of the land. If people don't like the fact that this is a secular nation, then tough. It is not acceptable for people to walk around this country with their faces covered. If I see someone with their face covered, I consider them to be either a bank robber, a terrorist or a mugger. Anyone wanting to live like that should go to another country, not live here. It isn't acceptable. It isn't part of British culture. If you live in Britain, why would you want to wear clothes that make it look as if you're living in the Middle East? It looks as if you don't enjoy living here. It makes for a more tense society.

I say again: this isn't racism. How rude would it be if a British person went to another country and ate only roast beef and Yorkshire pudding, and only ever wore a suit and a tie? See how barmy that would be?

To those who argue that immigrants who bring their country's customs with them add to the melting pot of multicultural Britain, I say: I can't stand multiculturalism. There's no such thing in my view. Multiracialism, yes. I'm a complete mongrel myself. Part Welsh, part Scots and a bit of English thrown in. But multiculturalism? It's bollocks.

Immigrants shouldn't be allowed to try to recreate the country they've left. That wouldn't be allowed anywhere else. We should permit people to keep their own ethnicity, but ensure they adopt 'Britishness'. My definition of that word would be fair play, understanding and a tolerance for anyone and everything, as long as it doesn't disrupt our society.

This should be the first item on any government's political agenda.

Let's reclaim this country for its own inhabitants. For the endangered species.

For people like me.

Now I was working at Talk Radio, I used to live in London during the week, then drive up to Harrogate at weekends. When I got there, I used to help out in the restaurant we'd established. It was called The Italian Connection. It was little more than a coffee shop to begin with, but we took over the lease and my son Peter started doing the cooking there. I was the wine waiter. People would come in and chat to me about the radio show or whatever I'd been doing, and I'd tell them about the variety of wonderful wines we stocked.

One night in 1998, I was halfway back up the M1 when I got a phone call from Melinda.

'Your mum's been taken to hospital,' she said.

My mum's boyfriend, Bill, with whom she'd lived for about ten years by that time, had rung to tell us the news. He was demanding that I went down to Wales to see her.

'I've just driven halfway from London,' I protested. 'I don't want to turn round and drive down to Wales now.'

'You mustn't,' Melinda told me. 'I've spoken to the hospital and they said there's nothing you can do even if you go there. Get a good night's sleep and go down tomorrow.'

The following day, I rang Bill.

Now, it's weird when your mum has a new man in her life. You kid yourself that you'll be grown up about things, but the fact is, that man with your mother is not your dad. He isn't the man who brought you up and there's always a little bit of friction, no matter how hard you try to prevent it. By this time, my dad had been dead for almost twenty years, so I was really happy for my mum that she'd found this new guy. I wanted her to find someone, but he wasn't Dad. Stating the obvious, I know, but that's just the way it was. There was never a connection between Bill and me. I used to go down to south Wales regularly to visit my mum and I tried really hard, for her sake, but it just didn't work.

So, this particular morning, Bill starts yelling down the phone: 'Don't you care about your mother? You've got to come and see her now.'

I thought this was typical Bill behaviour. After my mum started living with Bill, he took to ringing me up every year at the appropriate time to say: 'Don't forget it's your mother's birthday.' That used to really piss me off. My mum had been my mum for forty-odd years. I knew when her birthday was – it's only a few days after mine.

Anyway, I spoke to the doctor myself to find out how my mum was getting on.

'If you can come in the next few days, that'll be fine,' the doctor told me.

'What's wrong?' I wanted to know.

'I'm afraid she's got lung cancer,' he said.

Recently, my mum had been suffering with asthma.

She smoked every day, all her life. That may have been the trigger. Who knows? So many things can cause cancer, I don't think you can point the finger at one particular thing.

For the next couple of months, I did the longest commute of my life. I used to leave the radio station in London and drive to south Wales to see my mum; then drive up to Harrogate to see my wife; then drive back down to London again. I did that for three months and I was knackered.

I saw my mum as much as I could as the end drew near. Bill, meanwhile, had moved into her hospital room. He started sleeping on the floor. The staff asked if I could make him go home. He was absolutely besotted with my mother.

My main regret is that I never got any time on my own with my mum towards the end. But what chance did I have? Bill was always there. I know he loved her, but he seemed never to allow me or my brother or our wives to have any time alone with Mum before the end.

Finally, I got a phone call at about two o'clock one morning, to tell me that she'd died.

I went in the following day and Bill wanted to know why I hadn't come to the hospital as soon as I knew she was dead. I bit my tongue and didn't argue with him. Under the circumstances, it seemed the most dignified thing to do.

The time came to clear out her things from the house and I went through them all, but I couldn't find her will. So, I asked Bill about it. He couldn't tell me anything. He wasn't trying to hide things from me; he just couldn't cope.

'Who's her solicitor?' I asked him.

'I can't handle this now,' he told me. He disappeared. Walked out and vanished. I don't know where he went, but I appreciated that he clearly needed time on his own.

It turned out that Mum's will was with a solicitor in Bridgend, but my brother Keith and I didn't know which one. We had to walk round every single solicitor's office in this town, about a dozen of them, asking if my mother was their client. Finally, we found the right one. Subsequently, we learned that my mum had actually put a clause in her will leaving everything to me and my brother – and nothing to Bill, because he was already looked after.

Things just got confusing after that. Keith and I were told by the solicitor that we'd have to sell my mother's house. I don't know what Bill thought about it all. He'd turn up every now and then, before disappearing once more to God knows where. We were advised by the solicitor to change the locks on the house to comply with our mother's wishes, which I still find difficult to understand. It all became very undignified. We didn't want to make Bill homeless, after all. He just wouldn't talk to us, though. My mother had always asked us to include Bill, but he wasn't making it easy.

Bill reappeared for Mum's funeral. Just turned up and sat in the front row, not speaking to any of us. My brother read a lesson at the service and said a few words about her, then she was cremated.

Keith and I became much closer after Mum's death. We hadn't been that close as kids. Keith was the one with all the brains, so he'd won a scholarship and gone to a private school, while I'd attended the local secondary modern and left with few qualifications. My brother's had a proper job all his life, working for a pharmaceutical company. He's since emigrated to New Zealand. I miss him.

I got a call a few months later from the undertaker.

'Your mum's ashes are still here,' he told me. 'What would you like to do with them?'

I spoke to Keith and told him that I wanted to sprinkle her ashes in the sea in Porthcawl, where she'd gone back to after our dad had died, where she'd really loved being. She used to swim off the rocks opposite a hotel called The Seabank. It seemed the perfect thing to do for her. Keith agreed.

I went down to Wales on my own, collected the ashes and headed for the ocean. I placed the urn on the front seat of my car, telling my mum that I was taking her for a ride before I released her. Finally, I reached my planned destination. I clambered down on to the rocks and sat there for a while, looking out to sea and thinking about Mum. I got quite a lot of peace from that act. Then it was time.

'See you, Mum,' I said, and took the lid off the urn.

Suddenly, there was a tremendous gust of wind that blew the ashes everywhere – and I promptly swallowed a large proportion of my mother!

I sat on the rocks, hysterical with laughter. That, I thought, had completed the circle. My mother had given birth to me and now I'd swallowed her.

Am I completely crazy? Sometimes I think so.

There were three or four changes of management at Talk Radio after I joined. The station bumped along until we were finally taken over by the same people that owned Atlantic 252. I thought everything was going to be great. Unfortunately, I was wrong. They lost their way as well and we got yet more new owners in November 1998. This time, it was a consortium led by Kelvin MacKenzie, the legendary editor of *The Sun*. Talk Radio would never be the same again.

Most of my colleagues assumed that we were all going to be sacked and started looking for other jobs. I'd never met Kelvin MacKenzie and I had no idea what he might have thought of me. He himself is quite loud and brash, but then again, so can I be.

He came in and changed all kinds of things at the station. The presenter Anna Raeburn headed for the hills – though amazingly (in my opinion, as I found her very boring and patronizing), she's still on the radio elsewhere. She used to do the programme before me. I used to come on air and say: 'Thanks to Anna Raeburn for warming up the audience, and now, *The James Whale Show*.'

I thought it was quite funny, but I know Anna didn't agree. I thought she took herself far too seriously. She was only a glorified agony aunt, after all, and as far as I'm concerned, there is only one of those – and that's the delightful, fabulous Denise Robertson. Whether she's on TV or radio, Denise is warm and wonderful.

Kelvin was an interesting chap. He told you whether he liked you or not. Some people hated that, but I always thought that was fair enough. He'd put his own money into the station, after all. He knew what he wanted. He clearly liked me as I ended up doing a show from eight in the evening until one in the morning, increasing the length of my broadcast from three to five hours.

Kelvin gave the prats who work in radio a real wake-up call. He'd never worked in radio before. He brought in people he'd worked with previously to help him sort out Talk Radio – people like Mike Parry and Bill Ridley, the latter of whom is still programme director to this day, and whom, I'm very happy to say, has deservedly been named Programmer of the Year 2007 at the Arqiva Commercial Radio Awards. What the three of them did was take the station by the balls and give it a great big shaking. It was the best thing that could have happened.

Bill Ridley and I had a bit of a falling out when he first came on board. Bill had asked me to do something that I was certain wouldn't work. Annoyed, I went to see Kelvin MacKenzie.

'Look, I've been asked to do this and it's just going to make me look a fool,' I told him.

So, Kelvin and I talked, came to some kind of understanding and I left his office. I was walking along the corridor when I saw Bill Ridley coming the other way.

'Come into my office!' he shouted. 'Have you gone over my head to see Uncle?' (Kelvin was always referred to as Uncle.)

'He's the boss, it's his radio station,' I told Bill.

The argument escalated.

'Right,' I said. 'I'm going. You find someone else. I'm out of here.'

With that, I walked out of Bill's office and, as far as I was concerned, out of Talk Radio. Bill came after me.

'Listen, this is not a hill to die for,' he told me.

That phrase has always stuck in my mind for some reason.

I turned and went back into his office. We talked for ages and we cleared the air. No grudges were held. No revenge was planned. We acted like adults.

That's something a lot of the people I've met in radio over the years have been incapable of doing. In fact, it's probably one of the reasons I'm still working with Bill. It's great to have a programme director who backs you up. Bill is one of the few I've encountered who does that – even if I'm in the wrong. I'll get a bollocking, but he still supports me and I respect him for that. In broadcasting, you need to be fairly near the line and you need to know that the people employing you are prepared to stand up for you. You put yourself in a fairly invidious position and it can happen. As you probably already know, I've been the subject of numerous investigations by radio watchdogs (such as Ofcom, the Radio Authority and the Broadcasting Standards Commission) during my career in this industry. It makes the world of difference to have the backing of your station and programme director at those times. Even if the decisions go against you, if the station supported your right to express yourself in the course of your work, then that's really important. Whenever I go on air, I walk a fine line between what these watchdogs find acceptable and what they don't. I've had some crazy decisions made against me, and some that I perhaps deserved. On occasion, I've even been vindicated.

Just after Kelvin took over, I was the subject of one of these watchdog inquiries, when I had a go at a Scots listener who'd rung into the show. That night, I'd been my usual provocative self and opened up the phone lines for the audience to discuss whether Scotland and Wales would be anything without England. I always try to pick topics for my show that will provoke debate, and this was a particularly inflammatory subject. This caller was pro-Scotland himself, obviously, and he was very rude about both England and me. I wanted the opportunity to refute his comments, but the guy hung up. He wasn't prepared to listen to what I had to say in defence of this nation. Now, that's frustrating. The whole point of my show is to debate issues, not for one person to state their point of view and for that to be an end to the discussion.

So, I expressed this vexation on air – with a rant against the caller that maybe got a little too personal. I called him a wanker and said that he was thick, stupid, dirty and a verminous swine. In my defence, I do think my listeners also felt annoyed that this guy had walked away from the debate. Everybody wants a discussion to be a two-way process, and I think we all felt cheated that it had been one-sided in this instance.

In due course, I found that the caller had reported me to the Radio Authority. There was a claim that there appeared to be 'a strong current of racism towards the Scots running through the station', as *The Herald* reported at the time. Well, that's bollocks – something I'm glad to say the Radio Authority agreed with me on. I am not, nor have I ever been, racist. I find it ridiculous that I was accused of that charge – particularly because I'm part Scots and part Welsh myself. The Radio Authority fully cleared Talk Radio and me of the racism slur, and rightly so.

They found that my rant had been 'ill-judged'. All I can say is that I'm never going to be able to call it correctly every time. As a radio presenter, I have to face these kinds of choices every second I'm on air – when to take things further, when to sit back, when to be inflammatory, when I can tease or provoke callers. I'd be amazed if anyone was able to make the right decision on every occasion. I thought at the time that I'd been justified in saying what I did, but I accept that others thought differently.

Talk Radio were brilliant throughout all this. They were delighted when the Radio Authority's verdict was delivered, saying, 'This was James Whale in a typically strident mood. We are pleased that the Radio Authority has considered we are not anti-Scottish.' Good on them.

Lots of different shows passed through Talk Radio during this time, one of which was Kelvin's idea that my programme should be preceded by a different show every night. All sorts of journalist friends of his were subsequently shunted into the spot before me – and none of them worked. Sorry, Kelvin. They were rubbish. In the end, he realized he'd have to scrap the idea.

He and I were in the kitchen at Talk Radio one evening, at the Oxford Street studios.

'Why is it,' Kelvin wanted to know, 'that some of the top journalists in the country aren't working on this station?'

'Because they're not verbal communicators,' I told him. 'They've got crappy voices. They don't sound passionate. They might be able to write brilliantly, but when they open their mouths, they sound like morons.'

Kelvin went off to consider this fact and decided, eventually, that I was right. He liked to dabble, to change things, and the thing about radio is that you need to give it time. People get used to radio shows after a couple of years. You can put on a TV show and it can be a success in a day or a week. Same with books. Not so with radio. It's a different medium. It has different rules and it's governed by a completely different set of criteria. Radio is something people need time to get used to. You need stability. You can't just chop and change all the time, but it was Kelvin's money. It was Kelvin's station.

The thing I liked about Kelvin was that you always got feedback from him. If he liked you, he'd tell you; if he hated you, he'd tell you. After all, you can't work in a vacuum. You have to have some kind of feedback from someone other than your own listeners. Kelvin MacKenzie gave that kind of feedback – whether it was wanted or not.

On my Talk Radio show, as I'd done on all my previous TV and radio programmes, I included the behind-the-scenes team on the air. I've always involved the technicians and floor directors and sound men in what I do. When I was on TV, I'd chat to the cameramen. On the radio, I used to talk to the people who answered the phones and the station security guards and make them part of the programme. It didn't matter to me that they weren't miked up properly or that you couldn't hear exactly what they said. On the radio, it was all part of the theatre of the mind: it made the audience imagine who these people were and what they were like. It forced listeners to use their imaginations. It added a whole new dimension to the show.

Other people in radio have tried to copy this kind of thing. People like Steve Wright and Chris Moyles have a team of people who are there just for them to bounce off. But in most commercial radio, you can't afford the luxuries they have on the BBC. There just isn't the cash available that there is in some funded organization like the BBC. That's why some of their DJs work with teams of people. On my own programme, I have one person who books the guests and then I have Ash at night, during the show (so to speak).

Ash is my engineer and producer: a key component of my programme. We've worked together for years, ever since the late nineties. My first two engineers and producers at talkSPORT (as Talk Radio had now been renamed) were lovely, then I got Ash. I threaten to sack him every single night on the show. I abuse him verbally, but people seem to like the relationship we have. When Ash is on top form, he's very funny – so much so that a lot of listeners think he's a paid actor who's pretending to be the engineer, and that he's there just as a fall guy to make me look good. That's not the case. Ash operates the equipment in the main studio, he's the phone operator and he makes the tea. He isn't an actor. He's a real person doing real jobs. If you were to give

Ash a script, he wouldn't be funny. Sometimes he's difficult to control and sometimes he doesn't know when to shut up, but he has a natural wit that is perfect for the programme.

One of many possible examples of Ash's contribution to the show comes from around this time in the nineties. On this particular night, the guest was Heather Mills (before she married Paul McCartney). She'd been in a few times before as a guest, and she was good value. That evening, she was talking about her breast reduction.

'You know, man, they look the same size to me,' Ash remarked.

I thought it might be a good idea to get Ash's input on this, so I invited him into the studio, where, during the show, he proceeded to inspect Heather Mills's breasts carefully (with her consent, naturally), all the time relaying to the listeners their quality. So, Ash can actually say that he had his hands on Heather Mills's boobs long before Paul McCartney. What more could a man want?

Ash was also with me on the night in 1998 when the police tried to clear the studio because of a bomb threat somewhere outside. We were on air and a policeman came into the station to tell us that there'd been a bomb warning in the street outside and that we had to evacuate the building. Well, I had no intention of leaving in the middle of a show. The policeman was still trying to convince me when we came back on the air after a commercial break. The listeners were then treated to the sound of Ash, this policeman and me arguing about why we should or shouldn't get out of the Talk Radio building. We refused to leave, reasoning we were safer inside if the bomb was outside. The fact that Ash refused to give his name to the officer didn't really help matters, but that's just Ash for you. The police finally relented and we stayed inside.

Some people would call that being stubborn. I call it dedication. Of course, there are others who'd call it pig-headed stupidity. I suppose they could also be right.

Over the years, people have questioned the purpose and validity of shows like mine. Usually pillocks who've tuned in once by accident and heard something that they didn't like, something that offended their delicate sensibilities. But to question my programme and those like it is to question the need to talk and communicate. Surely we're all here on this planet to contribute in some small way to a grand plan. Perhaps, in some cases, simply talking is contribution enough.

People need to talk. If they talked more, we wouldn't have so many bloody wars. If governments talked instead of getting their armies to shoot at each other, then the world would be a more peaceful place. If people communicated more, then the country wouldn't be in such a state. If talk were the natural form of interaction between individuals, then perhaps there'd be less violence in day-to-day society. People seem to have lost the ability to speak to each other. I hope that programmes like mine may give them that ability once again. People need to communicate more and they need a forum in which to do it. The talk-radio show provides that forum. At its best, it can stimulate debate and discussion. At its most base, it is simply entertainment – and, surely, all of us listen to the radio or watch TV to be entertained in some way, shape or form.

Moreover, my show serves another, far more

important function – one that is all too easily overlooked. I'm not going to launch into some expansive lecture about why programmes like mine are so necessary; I'd rather give you an example, from 1999, of how they can help people.

I was interviewing Sir Ian McKellen on this particular day. It was not long after his film *Gods and Monsters* had been released. He was talking about gay issues. Sir Ian is gay and a strong supporter of gay rights. During the show, a young lad rang in. He couldn't have been more than sixteen or seventeen. He wanted to speak to Sir Ian about coming out. This lad had been living in fear of his family's reaction to his announcement. He rang in hoping to get some advice from Sir Ian on how to tackle the problem.

The call and the initial conversation went out on the show, but then Sir Ian stayed on the line with this lad while we went into a break. He talked to him, advised him and reassured him, but the youngster still didn't seem too enthusiastic about how his family might react. Finally, he rang off.

We continued with the show. As Ash was feeding me more calls, he announced that the same young lad was back on the line. It was about an hour later. The lad sounded completely different. The tone of his voice had changed from what had sounded like grim resignation to something like happiness.

'I taped our conversation,' he said to Sir Ian. 'I taped what you said to me and played it back to my family. Everything is fine.'

He told us that his family were all with him now and they were delighted for him; everyone was hugging each other. You could hear the relief in his voice.

I looked across at Sir Ian and there were tears of joy rolling down his cheeks.

The lad thanked us both for taking the call and put down the phone.

It's one of the best examples I can think of where just talking has helped someone with problems. That young man had no one else to talk to. He had nobody else with whom he could share his problems and concerns, so he rang the show. He communicated.

So, some people might find the show offensive, some might find me objectionable and opinionated. Fortunately, for everyone who has that view, there are hundreds more who listen and get something positive from the programme. Either help, inspiration, a new way of looking at a topic, or just a bit of entertainment.

I am convinced by the power of positive thought: a power that my radio show helps to build. I like to think that the forum the show provides may give the listeners some comfort. It might help them to face a problem or it might give them the strength to understand how to cope.

Little did I know it then, but I was about to have to call on that strength myself. Life had one of its nasty surprises lying in store for me, and everything was about to change.

It was a beautiful crisp winter's morning, the day I found out I was going to die. They say that human beings are the only animals able to contemplate their own mortality. It was just that, at the age of forty-eight, I didn't expect to be doing such a thing.

I'd spent the morning sitting at the bottom of the Oxo Tower on the banks of the River Thames, talking to Derek Hatton. Derek had his own show on talkSPORT, where I was still working, and I'd been giving him a few tips and pointers on broadcasting. In fact, I'd encouraged him to go into radio in the first place. I'd interviewed him some time before and told him he was a natural for the medium.

So, we were sitting having a coffee and enjoying a very pleasant morning. I mentioned to Derek that I was due to receive the results of a check-up I'd had with a specialist, concerning some problems with my kidneys. I'd been having trouble with what I guessed to be kidney stones and had undergone a series of tests to pin down the problem. Derek, a genial Scouser, jovially assured me that he too had suffered from kidney problems and that he was sure everything would be all right.

So, with that assurance ringing in my ears, I walked off to the hospital, still enjoying the beautiful weather and feeling very much at peace with myself and the world in general. The hospital was fifteen minutes' walk away and it seemed the perfect morning to take a stroll.

Eventually, I arrived at the clinic, took my place in the waiting room and waited my turn, lazily flicking through the magazines and newspapers, my mind not even particularly occupied with the impending results. The specialist, a man named Tim O'Brien, came out and asked me to come into his office.

Still smiling, I walked into Tim's office, expecting him to have a course of tablets ready for me to take to rid me of my kidney stones. At worst, I was worried that he might inform me that I would have to have minor surgery to have them removed. Being self-employed, I didn't want to take too much time off work and had previously discussed with Tim the possibility of curing the problem without surgery. He'd been quite happy to consider that option.

'So, go on,' I said, cheerily. 'Hit me. Tell me the worst.'

Without the slightest hesitation – and the words will remain with me for the rest of my life – Tim said, 'James, I'm very sorry. You've got a tumour on one of your kidneys and, I have to tell you, it's the biggest tumour I've ever seen.'

I jokingly told him that I didn't want any chemotherapy; I didn't want to lose any more hair. I asked the sort of questions I thought you should ask, including the inevitable one. A question I'm sure anyone in the same situation must need an answer for. I asked him how long I had to live.

'I have to be honest with you,' he told me. 'Never having seen a tumour this big before, I have no idea. I can't tell you the exact prognosis, but I want to send you now for a complete scan to see how far the cancer has spread.'

It was the first time he had used the word 'cancer' and it hit me with an impact I didn't think one single word was capable of. When cancer is mentioned, one immediately equates it with words like 'malignant', 'inoperable' and 'terminal'. When that word is spoken in the office of a specialist, possibly even more so on the kind of beautiful sunny morning it was that day, it carries a power and gravitas that is indescribable. To hear the word 'cancer' really brought home to me how ill I was.

What was curious was that leading up to the diagnosis, I had felt fine. A little tired, perhaps, but I had put that down to the fact that Melinda and I were preparing to move from our home in Harrogate to a flat in London (the one I lived in while doing the show on talkSPORT). I'd simply thought the pressures of the planned move had been catching up with me. I'd also just completed a twenty-four-hour edition of my radio show, done live from the Millennium Dome on New Year's Eve 1999, so I hadn't equated my fatigue with anything other than a combination of these two things.

Admittedly, I'd had a pee one morning and seen my urine was bright red, but neither Melinda nor I put this down to anything serious. In fact, Melinda joked that, due to the amount of sex we'd had on the long overdue holiday we'd just returned from, she may have, as she put it, 'broken it'. A variety of tests had come up with little to suggest that I was suffering from anything other than a slight kidney problem, possibly kidney stones. Even the undignified, uncomfortable and unpleasant ordeal of an endoscope exploring my bladder had revealed no problems, so to be suddenly told that I was stricken with cancer was a blow I could never have envisaged.

Tim's first priority was to see how far the cancer had spread. Once that fact had been established, we would speak again, he said.

'Your wife's up in Yorkshire, isn't she?' he continued. 'Why don't you ring her and ask her to come down? I'd like to see both of you on Friday morning.'

By this time, I was feeling more than a little shell-shocked. I prepared to go off for a CT scan that would pinpoint more accurately the size and spread of the cancer. I asked Tim if I could have the results immediately. It already felt as if time was simultaneously whizzing past and moving at half-speed. I couldn't think straight. This was the first time I'd even been in hospital as an adult. I'd had a grumbling appendix when I was four or five, but other than that, I'd never been inside for so much as an overnight stay.

I had the scan and, just to compound my worry, they didn't tell me the results. I left, still numb, and walked the ten minutes or so back to my flat. My mood couldn't have been more different from how it had been earlier that morning, when the world had seemed such a wonderful place and I had felt so alive. I sat in my chair and looked out of the window of the flat, gazing blankly at the panoramic views of London, views I possibly had only a limited time to enjoy. I sat and sat, just wondering what the hell I was going to do. The only thought that kept going through my mind was

'Melinda is going to be furious'. I'm not sure why I thought that – it's surprising, the kinds of things that go through your mind when you're faced with your own possible demise.

I was also aware that I needed to let people know what had happened. I thought about all the people I should call, not really sure what the hell I was going to say to them when they answered their phones. Finally, I decided that Melinda was the person I should ring first. It might seem strange that I felt there was a decision to make. Looking back on it, perhaps I was trying to spare her the news for as long as I could. If I rang other people and told them, at least Melinda would be blissfully ignorant of my condition for just that little bit longer … but then I realized that if I spoke to other people and someone else informed her of the diagnosis, then the shock would be twice as bad. Also, if she ever found out that I had told someone else before her, then she would be devastated.

There have been a number of occasions in my life when, for different reasons, I've been frightened, but reaching for the phone that afternoon was the worst by far. I had no idea how Melinda was going to react. I knew that she loved me and that I loved her, even though I knew I didn't tell her that often enough (like most husbands). I just hope that she realizes now how much I do love her.

So, I rang her.

'How was it?' she wanted to know. 'What did the doctor say?'

'He thinks I've got cancer,' I told her.

There was a silence, and then she said: 'You must be joking.' The words just exploded out of her mouth.

I told her again, and the realization began to hit her as surely as it had hit me. I asked her if she could come down on Friday for the meeting with Tim, when he would reveal the prognosis. She asked me to give her a minute to digest what she'd just heard, and said she would then ring me back. What I discovered later was that she had been speechless with shock, and was unable to say anything more to me because she was crying. She literally couldn't say a word; her speech had totally dried up.

So, I sat waiting for the phone to ring, feeling a little like the condemned man in the electric chair, waiting for the governor's final call that will either reprieve or damn him. I was again consumed by thoughts of what I was going to do and whom I was going to have to tell. Also, how I was going to tell them. It isn't easy, finding the words to express such facts. A curious thing: that I should find it so difficult to find the words, when words, throughout my career, have always been the tools of my trade.

It wasn't until then that I actually cried. The realization, the fear, and possibly even the anger poured out of me and I wept, which was probably a good thing to do.

The phone rang and it was Melinda.

'Right,' she said. 'The first thing we've got to do is tell James and Peter. You ring James; I'll ring Peter. I'll be with you in London by ten tonight, once I've had the dog taken to the kennels. What are you going to do?'

I told her I was going to go into work, as usual. It never occurred to me that I wouldn't.

I next rang my son, James, and attempted to explain to him what I'd heard earlier that day from the doctor. I rang my brother Keith and I rang Stuart, my agent, who was totally shocked – but I swore him to secrecy. I didn't want anyone else to know, especially people in the business.

Meanwhile, Melinda had rung Mike, a friend of ours, and asked him to look after me. Of course, I protested that I didn't need looking after, that it was, after all, only cancer. I felt fine. I didn't need a minder. Regardless, Mike duly arrived and suggested we go out for a meal and have a few drinks. We did so and I drank two or three bottles of wine, which had no apparent effect. I then went into talkSPORT to do my show. I told no one there. Not even Ash, my producer and engineer. I did the programme. It's amazing how learning that you may be terminally ill concentrates your mind. I got through the show without a hiccup (if you'll excuse the phrase, considering how much wine I'd drunk) and still no one around me knew. I must have been pissed, but no one noticed.

What that says about the standard of my show, I'm not sure, but I got through it.

I don't know why I didn't want any work colleagues to know – perhaps I was afraid they'd try to get me off the air. Perhaps I thought they'd be afraid that I'd start telling my listeners about the news I'd received that morning. Talking about cancer on the radio is never good for ratings.

By this time, Melinda had arrived in London, so Mike picked her up and said that he was going to take her out and cheer her up. Having cried all the way down on the train, she certainly needed something to help her through the next few hours. Mike took her to a gay bar, which was hosting male strippers that night. It had the desired effect, because she was considerably more cheerful by the time she met me later that night, well after midnight.

We spent Thursday worrying and talking, speaking on the phone to one or two other people about what I knew so far. Again, that night I did my show, still telling no one what was wrong. Even without the aid of three bottles of wine, I got through it without a problem.

Friday finally dawned and Melinda and I were up early to see Tim O'Brien for the results of the tests. I have to confess, I didn't sleep much the night before and I'm sure Melinda didn't either. Night-time was always the worst, because it gave me more time to think and to run through everything in my mind that was or might be happening to me. By this time, I will admit, I was fearing the worst. I had told Tim that I didn't really want to have an operation; Tim wasn't even sure if an operation would be an option. I could have months, or even less, to live. To say that my head was spinning would be an understatement.

At last, we went in to see Tim, who first had a chat with Melinda to put her fully in the picture, then he told us both the rest.

'The scan has come back,' he said, 'and the cancer doesn't seem to have spread anywhere else, which is very good news. Let me show you some of the pictures we've taken of the tumour.'

Well, it looked the same colour and size as a medium mushroom pizza. There was no kidney to be seen.

I asked Tim why I hadn't felt pain from such a huge tumour, and he proceeded to tell me that it hadn't infected any other regions of my body, and that it also hadn't come into conflict with any others. I may well have had this thing growing inside me for five years. Tim suggested an operation. Without one, there was no chance of survival. Believe it or not, I was still reluctant to take that step. I hadn't enjoyed my time in hospital with a grumbling appendix as a child; I didn't want to come back in. My reluctance was magnified when Tim explained the procedure necessary for removing the tumour. I was to be cut from beneath my arm, across to my opposite hip, almost cutting me in half.

I sat somewhat dumbly while Melinda asked the relevant questions. It was, I guess, what an out-of-body experience must feel like: I was in that office, but everything seemed to be going on around me. Tim confessed that he didn't know what the tumour was attached to, or even if he could get it out. I had a fifty-fifty chance, at best, of surviving the operation.

'What are my chances of fully recovering?' I asked.

He told me 40 per cent. He also told me he'd have to be assisted by another consultant, that my spleen might well have to be removed. He told me lots of other things, but I didn't really hear them. I had a 50 per cent chance of dying during the operation and a 40 per cent chance of survival afterwards. Now, I'm not a betting man, but these odds didn't seem too encouraging to me, though I wasn't really in a position to bargain. Tim told us that he had to go away for a week, but that, after cross-matching my blood and tissue, he would perform the operation to remove both the tumour and my kidney the following Monday.

Still in a state of shock, we left the office. Melinda seemed fairly upbeat. Prior to that meeting, she said, we had been given very little hope; at least we now had some. I was still more concerned about having to spend time in hospital. My mind was already crammed with facts, half of which I didn't understand, the other half I didn't want to contemplate.

Amidst the fog of medical jargon, I now had just one luminous thought in my mind. I knew what I wanted and where I wanted to go. At last, I knew what I had to do and I set about doing it right there and then.

Melinda and I got in our car and drove to Brighton. We checked into the Grand Hotel, where I requested a suite. I didn't care how much it cost.

It's funny how, when you've just been given a death sentence, money suddenly doesn't mean anything. I certainly didn't want to die leaving any.

Inside our suite, we ordered some wine and got absolutely paralytic. Then we went for a walk. Once we got back to the hotel, I rang my agent and asked him to ring everyone who needed to know about my illness. I now wanted him to tell them what was going on.

I sat in our room, looking out at the sea. It was like looking out into infinity. I now understand why some people want to go to the ocean when their time comes. It draws you. Perhaps it's some kind of deep-rooted shared memory that all of mankind possesses. We came from the water millions of years ago and perhaps there's a universal desire to return to it when death looms.

It's nothing at all to do with my name being Whale, I promise you.

I received lots of calls from people, everyone very upset and emotional, but the call that I remember with the most warmth was from my boss at talkSPORT, Kelvin MacKenzie.

'I've got Kelvin on the line for you,' his secretary said.

I was astonished. Even though I worked for this man, I didn't see him very often and he's also not the kind of man with whom you make small talk, so I was surprised by the call.

'What the fuck's going on?' snapped the rough voice at the other end of the line. 'You can't be ill. You can't have time off. Your programme's the only one that's got any listeners. I'll have to close the station down and, if I do, it'll be your fault.'

This is Kelvin's way and it made me laugh.

'Sorry, mate, I really am,' I answered. 'I feel bad about it.'

'Don't worry about it,' he told me. 'Whatever you need. Money. Anything. If people do right by me, then I do right by them. I want you back on the air in six weeks. You'll be all right.'

That was the best phone call and the best approach that I could have had at that time. Right away, it made me feel much better.

That night, unsurprisingly, I couldn't sleep. I got up in the darkness and sat in an armchair, just looking out over the sea. I needed to make plans of some kind. I had no idea how long I had left to live. I had to make arrangements.

I decided that I was going to take some time off work before the operation. That shocked Kelvin, I know. I think he was expecting me to go back and work right up until I was taken into the operating theatre.

I just wanted to get things in order. I wanted to

know that Melinda would be all right once I'd gone. That she'd have somewhere to live and be looked after. I hadn't planned for this. Who does? You never think about this kind of thing, naturally, unless you're in a position where you have to. I had to work out if I had enough insurance, whether I could clear some of our debts and other things that you never even think of.

Also, I wanted to tell the listeners of my show that I had cancer. I wanted to tell them while I was on the air; tell them what was wrong with me and that I'd be going away for a while.

The following week, I spoke to Bill Ridley, the programme director.

'Bill,' I said. 'If I go on and say I've got cancer and this is my last show, but hopefully some time in the future I'll be back, then there'll be some people jumping up and down, thinking "great", but there'll be others ringing in the following day, wondering if they heard right. I want to find a newspaper to do the story.'

A young lady from *The Sun* came along and they did a lovely story about it all.

I announced the situation to my loyal listeners on 14 February 2000. What a valentine. The listeners were great. They helped me to believe in the power of positive collective thought. One of the things that really boosted me before I had the operation was people ringing in, saying, 'I had cancer of the kidney years ago, and I'm all right.'

A fifteen-year-old rang in and told me he'd had cancer and got over it. 'You'll be all right, mate,' he added.

I have a love–hate relationship with my audience and I know that I wind people up and say some extreme things. Nevertheless, I've always thought that my regular listeners understood me – though I certainly didn't expect the response I got to that edition of the show. Flowers, cards and letters of goodwill flooded in, and I'm convinced they all aided my recovery. I was overwhelmed by the support. I am so grateful to all the listeners who rang in to express their good wishes and their hopes for me. Admittedly, about half a dozen of the messages were from people who said they were glad I'd got cancer – but then, you can't please everyone, can you?

The vast majority were from people who were incredibly supportive. I'd assumed, because of the sort of personality I have, that a lot of people would have been glad to see the back of me, but obviously I must connect with a lot of people. I wish I could thank every one of those people individually for their kindness at that time. You never know, perhaps one day I will.

I did the programme for the final time (well, I hoped it wouldn't be ...) on the Monday before I was due to have my operation. The operation had been scheduled for Monday week. Melinda and I then went off to Yorkshire, to sort out what we were doing and also to resolve where I wanted to be if I came through the operation.

I decided I wanted to stay in London. I didn't want to be in the country. I wanted to be in the city, where everything was going on. If it was going to be the end of my life, I wanted to be there. I was lucky. I'd been well insured, so we paid off the mortgage on our house in Yorkshire. Melinda (as ever, it was Melinda who did the hard work) found us a place in the capital, as we decided my London flat would be too small for the two of us. Then, as we'd originally planned before all this happened, we moved from Yorkshire down to London.

A downside of the move was that we had to find a new home for our German shepherd dog, George. He was a brilliant pet, one of the family, but we had to find new owners for him. I think leaving George behind upset Melinda more than anything, but once again she showed how selfless she was. She did that for me, just as she'd done so much for me in the past. It's one of many things for which I'll never be able to repay her.

All too soon, these time-consuming arrangements had devoured the entire week I'd had stretching out before me, delaying my inevitable admission to hospital. Prior to my operation for the removal of the tumour, I'd never had an operation in my life, so I had no idea what to expect and was understandably nervous about the whole procedure.

I went to the hospital the day before the actual event for some final tests and X-rays. Melinda stayed with me until about eleven o'clock that night. I felt like a condemned man. People came to see me to wish me well; surgeons, doctors, nurses and anaesthetists wandered in periodically to talk to me. I filled in forms. It all passed in a bit of a blur, and I was glad they all went in the end. A certain sort of calm descended on me.

It must have been much worse for Melinda, and for all those not directly involved. They must have been the people who really suffered. When it's happening to you, you just deal with it. What choice do you have?

Finally, it was time for Melinda to leave. I wouldn't see her the next morning. She let Tim, my surgeon, know that she wouldn't be coming in. It wasn't a good idea, for many reasons. Firstly, I wouldn't even know whether she was there or not, as I'd be zonked out from the anaesthetic. Secondly, Melinda feared that she wouldn't be able to cope with seeing me, be that pre-op, or the unknown that awaited us both post-op. Tim promised he'd ring her as soon as the operation was over. So, Melinda headed home. I told her to take a cab, as she seemed absolutely done in with the stress of it all – but she later told me she'd just walked out of the hospital and gone home in a daze. She didn't get any sleep that night for worrying. In the morning, all she could do was sit at home, waiting for the phone to ring.

After Melinda had left, I had a long chat with the anaesthetist.

'Are you worried about anything?' he asked, with supreme understatement.

'I don't want to wake up in the middle of the operation,' I told him.

'People don't,' he assured me.

'Well, you hear that some people do,' I commented archly.

He told me everything would be fine. I had a shower and got back into bed to pass a very fitful night, despite the fact that one of the consultants had given me something to help me sleep.

The next morning, they came for me. I remember being wheeled into the operating theatre and all these people in blue gowns looking down at me.

'They all seem to be so very tall,' I thought.

That's the last thing I remember. I don't remember anything after that, until I woke up in intensive care. I remember Melinda was sitting beside the bed.

'It's all right,' she told me. 'They've got it all out. You're okay.'

At one point, later that night, I found a phone on the belt of one of the intensive-care nurses and I remember dialling my mobile and getting Melinda. In the background, there was the sound of raised voices and laughter.

'Where are you?' I asked, groggily. 'What are you doing?'

'We're all out celebrating,' she told me.

'Good,' I said, and went back to sleep. Exactly how I managed to dial the number in the first place, I have no idea.

I have one abiding memory of being in intensive care. During the operation, they'd had to deflate my lung to get the tumour out, and they'd had to put a huge tube in afterwards to re-inflate it. I remember them coming to remove that tube. I was still heavily sedated and unable to feel anything, but I remember watching a piece of clear piping about two feet long being removed from my torso. Once the medical team had finished, they used a huge curved needle that looked like an Arab warrior's scimitar to stitch me up.

I just remember smiling while they were pulling this tube out of my insides. Bizarre.

They eventually took me back to the general ward, and for the first day that I was there, I was unable to move or eat. But on the second day, they tried to get me out of bed. I couldn't believe it. I know the health service likes to get people on their feet again as quickly as possible after operations, but this was ridiculous.

'We've got to get you up now,' the physiotherapist told me.

'I'm going to be here for at least two weeks,' I thought.

I was wrong.

They made me stand up. I was looking out of the window and it was like everything outside suddenly rushed into my head and I passed out. As soon as my head touched the pillow, I was fine again. They said they'd be back in a couple of hours to try again. They were determined to get me out of that bloody bed.

Finally, they got me up. That battle had been bad enough, but now they told me they wanted me to walk. Needless to say, I did it in the end, carrying my piss-filled catheter bag with me. To this day, I wonder if I should have asked for a bag to match my shoes.

'The more you walk, the sooner you can go home,' they kept telling me.

It felt as if I was in there for ages, but I was actually in hospital for only ten days. Loads of people came to visit me, including Derek Hatton, who'd been with me the day of my first hospital appointment, when I'd found out what was wrong with me. Derek's a lovely bloke, but I couldn't get him to go. Here's a tip for any of you visiting someone in hospital: go regularly, but for only fifteen or twenty minutes at a time.

Mike Mansfield, my old TV producer, also came. He gave me a book about the supernatural. I don't know if he was trying to tell me something.

Now, I'm not a squeamish man, but I didn't like looking at the main wound on my body, the one that bisected my torso, one bit. It made me look as if I'd been in a samurai sword fight. I asked the nurse to keep the plaster on, but Tim came round one day and said, 'I want to see how the wound's getting on.'

I was sitting on a chair.

'We'll have that plaster off,' he told me and, with

that, he ripped the whole thing off in one go. I thought he'd just pulled my insides open again.

'I don't want to see that on again,' he said to me.

I looked down to see that the huge gash was held together not with stitches, but with metal staples. I thought I was going to pass out again.

Time went by and finally, despite my protests, it was the day I was due to go home. I didn't think I was well enough to leave the hospital, but everyone insisted I was fine. I was told to return a week later and they'd remove the staples.

That's what happened. The staples were duly removed and I set about getting my strength back. I prepared to carry on living my life. A life that, if not for Tim O'Brien, I wouldn't have.

My whole body had been under threat from the cancer, but what was about to happen next seemed likely to destroy my very sanity.

HOLD YOUR HORSES – THIS IS WHAT I THINK ...

UP YOURS, EQUALITY

I hate equality.

Why should we all be fucking equal?

Why on earth should we have to be equal? Why, if you earn more money, shouldn't you be able to improve your life through better education, better medicine? Why not? If you can't get better things because you have more money than someone else, what is the point of actually working hard? We might as well all be given a certain amount of money by the state and not bother to do anything else.

The drive for equality tries to make us all the same. Why would anyone want that to happen? When did individuality and originality become things to be stamped out and eradicated? It seems absolutely insane to me.

I hate everything being the same. I hate blandness. Every city, every town, every village that you go into these days: there are the same stores. There aren't individual shops with their own identities any more. You get your coffee from Starbucks or Costa or one of the other chains. You get your groceries from Sainsbury's or Asda or Morrisons. You get your clothes from Topshop or Next.

Everything is exactly the same. There is no more individuality and we are all in danger of being totally controlled. If we don't measure up, if we're not perceived to behave in exactly the right way, then we'll be shunned. We will become a nation of nonentities. We'll all look the same, dress the same, behave the same, eat the same – even think the same.

I'm fed up with it.

In the future, I expect we'll be born with no arms and legs. That way, we won't be able to offend anyone. We'll just be blobs. We'll just sit there and nod in agreement with whomever's pulling our strings at the time. We won't be allowed our own opinions or, if we are, we certainly won't be allowed to express them.

Of course, they say that this is a country of free speech. I say: absolute bollocks.

This country is one of free speech as long as you say what the majority are thinking. As long as you tow the party line. If you dare to have an opinion that is against the norm, or that makes you stand out from the crowd, then you're vilified or you're held up as some kind of lunatic.

No one wants to be different these days. That's why people are so frightened of confrontation. No one wants to have an argument because they're scared of upsetting someone. No one wants to express an opinion in case it makes people look at them.

They don't want to stand out from the crowd. That's why there's no rebellion in this country any more. The youth of today are so apathetic they wouldn't protest if someone locked them up in prison camps. They're so busy with their games consoles, their iPods and their mobile phones, they hardly know what's going on around them. The only time they get irate is when someone steals one of these gadgets from them.

Is this the same country that gave the world punk rock

back in the seventies? Punks might have looked ridiculous, but at least they preached rebellion. They encouraged youngsters to do more than sit on their backsides all day sending bloody text messages back and forth.

These days, as people grow up, they want the same as all their friends. They want what's shown to them in magazines like *OK!*, *Hello!* and *Heat*, and all the other rags devoted to talentless nobodies who spend their time going to every free party they get invited to. The magazines say: 'Dress like this celebrity. Look like this celebrity. Behave like this celebrity.'

No one is encouraged to have their own thoughts and views. All people do is copy the views of those people that the media hold up as role models.

Frankly, it's bloody frightening.

I'd been out of hospital for three or four months. I was getting my strength back and starting to enjoy life again. One afternoon, I was having a rest when the phone rang.

It was my son, Peter.

Like all parents, I was delighted to hear from one of my kids and asked him how he was. He was in bad shape. He was convinced that his wife was having an affair.

He'd rung me about this a couple of times before, and told me he suspected this was going on. I told him it was crazy talk, not to think about it and the usual sorts of things that a concerned father would say.

But it transpired that Peter was right. His wife was indeed having an affair. How long it had been going on for no one could be sure, but there was no mistaking the fact that she was cheating on him.

'She's left me,' Peter said now, almost hysterical. 'She's going away. I think she might take the children with her.'

Still I tried to be the voice of reason, but to no avail. He was distraught.

'It's no good, Dad,' he said. 'I've got to deal with it. I'll call you back.'

I put the phone down, a little shaken, wondering how the hell I could help him. As a parent, you never stop worrying about your kids, no matter how old they get. If they're suffering, you suffer too, and you'll do anything you can to help them.

I got another phone call from Peter a little later. He'd taken his son, one of his two children, down to the restaurant and phoned me from there.

'I'm not letting her take the kids,' he said. 'I've brought my son to work and I'm thinking about what's going on.'

'You'll have to take him home, sit down and discuss it,' I told him.

Peter did as I suggested and went back home with his son, with the intention of resolving the situation somehow.

Unfortunately, when he got home, the police were there.

My son was understandably extremely upset about this. His wife was the one having the affair, threatening to run off with her bit on the side – yet Peter was the one being confronted by the police. What his wife might have said to them no one knew, but they seemed to be intent on arresting Peter, presumably because they'd been told that he'd abducted his own son.

He was furious to the point that it took nine policemen to arrest him and get him into a police van. He ended up in the cells that night, but wasn't charged with anything.

I should say at this point that he's up in Yorkshire; I'm in London recovering from cancer. It wasn't a good time. If I'd been fit and healthy, I'd have been up there immediately. I'd have dropped everything to be at his side. Knowing me, I'd probably have ended up in the cell next to him.

Time went by. One day, Peter's wife rang me. 'Sorry for what's happened,' she said, 'but Peter and I never got on.' She trotted out every lame, clichéd excuse in the book. I just listened, trying to control my anger. Rightly or wrongly, I had the impression that she expected Peter to sell the restaurant business and give her half, but that was never going to happen.

It was so frustrating, knowing that there was nothing I could do. I spoke to Peter on the phone every day and he kept me in touch with the entire complicated mess. This thorny situation seemed to go on for an eternity – then suddenly Peter's wife, her new boyfriend and both the children left Yorkshire.

We didn't know where they were. Peter didn't know. As far as we were concerned, it was as if they'd vanished from the face of the earth. Even the police, who were involved in looking for the party, never found hide nor hair of them. A difficult situation quickly became intolerable.

They were missing for about a year. During this time, Peter was – unsurprisingly – going mad, tortured by thoughts of where his wife and kids might be. I can only imagine the mental torture he went through and I can fully understand how his only outlet for this pent-up rage and anguish was to take it out on himself. He had absolutely nowhere to turn.

His restaurant business, which Melinda and I also owned with him, was closed most of the time. Who can wonder at it? With Peter's life turned so comprehensively upside down, he could barely look after himself, let alone a business. We managed by hook and by crook to keep it going. We borrowed money and poured it into the restaurant in a frantic bid to save it from going under, though doing so almost bankrupted us. We did consider selling it, but Melinda and I both realized that if we did this, it would be the final nail in the coffin for Peter. He hadn't got much left, but if the restaurant went too, then he would have nothing to live for.

I hoped that he might move down to London to be with us, so we could support him more fully. He didn't want to leave Harrogate, though.

From a father's point of view, I cannot imagine the torments he went through. One night he was kissing his children goodnight, the next day he didn't even know where they were. He didn't know if they were safe, if they had enough to eat or if they were being mistreated. How he managed not to commit suicide, I'll never know. All I can think is that he must have inherited some of his mother's incredible mental strength and character. Lesser men would have crumbled completely. I respect him immensely for having had the will to get out of bed every day at that time, let alone to continue with his life in the way he has done.

By this time, I was back at work on talkSPORT. The first time I went back into the studio after my operation, I must have looked a right pillock. I walked in, bent over and hobbling. I went around to everyone and spoke to them, thanked them for their support and their kindness.

Bill Ridley had been asking Melinda for a while when I was going to return to work. She kept telling him it would be soon – but I was thinking never. I just hadn't got any anger. I couldn't get worked up about

anything. I didn't even think I was fit for Radio 2: it was
that bad.

I couldn't see how I was ever going to be the
person I used to be before the operation. Apart from
the obvious physical damage that the cancer had
caused, the whole process had taken something from
me psychologically, too. It had blunted any edge I'd
had. It had stifled the frustration I'd felt at many
things; not a good thing for someone who has made
his living for so many years by being contentious and
confrontational.

However, when Melinda and I had moved down to
London just before my operation, the new house we'd
purchased required another mortgage, which of course
meant that I *had* to keep working. Whatever my gut
instinct about going back to work, I couldn't just sit
around and fester at home, brooding on my experiences
and my huge scar. Looking back on it, I'm grateful that
I did have to continue working, because it gave me
something else to focus on, rather than just fretting
about my condition. Had I not gone back to work when
I did, I have no doubt that I would now be working in
the big Radio Station in the Sky.

I might have more listeners, of course.

In the end, I did go back to work. First one night a
week, then building up to four nights as I got stronger.
But the problem still remained. Had I lost my edge for
good? When was I going to find something to make me
angry again? The man who helped me get over all this
was the man who'd saved my life.

I invited Tim O'Brien, my surgeon, on to the show
one night and we did a kind of re-enactment of my
operation on air. It was a bit vulgar, but, somehow, it

got me back to my old self. After that show, I was back to my usual, tasteless, off-the-wall self again.

I used to say, 'The only thing that's going to make me feel better is a virgin rubbing her breasts over my scar.'

It didn't happen, but we can all dream, can't we?

Every night I said that, it offended someone. I felt I was getting back to normal at last. But one thing was far from normal: Peter's family situation. Every single night, I'd leave my mobile phone switched on during the show, and every night Peter would call me. I expected his calls. I knew how upset he was. He was in a terrible state.

I would sit doing my show at nights, being the same James Whale that everyone wanted to hear, and then during commercial breaks I would talk to my son. The façade would slip. I wasn't the 'hard man of the airwaves' when the microphones were off, I was just a dad who was desperate to help his son. The fact that I knew deep down I could do nothing made the situation even more unbearable.

Nevertheless, I talked to him. Reassured him it would all work out and told him not to do anything stupid. I don't know who I was trying the hardest to convince: Peter or myself.

I actually knew the guy my son's wife had run off with. I'd known him for about two years – only in passing and only to a degree as a business contact. He ran a car-leasing business and he used to get cars, periodically, for Melinda and me. I'd never really liked him. There was something about him that struck me as untrustworthy.

In time, we discovered that my ex-daughter-in-law

and her boyfriend were in France, with both the children. Unable to stand his pain any longer, Peter went there to try to sort things out. I was pleased that he did. As it turned out, his visit led to a temporary truce. Peter went to see them a couple of times in an attempt to resolve the problems. He was allowed to take his children for a holiday in the Pyrenees in the south-west of France, where they'd all been living. Melinda and I benefited, too: we joined them. We had a wonderful vacation in and around the town of Carcassonne. We took advantage of this fleeting time to enjoy the sort of contact with our grandchildren that we'd feared we might never have again.

Unfortunately, it didn't last long. It seemed to me that my ex-daughter-in-law just did not want to have Peter or us in their lives. How much of an influence her boyfriend was in all this I'll never know. What I do know is that he was extremely plausible, even persuasive. For me, it wasn't hard to understand how he'd managed to manipulate my son's family away from him.

Meanwhile, I was also worried about my other son, James. He'd had a bad time of it as well, coming to terms with the fact that one minute I was going to die, and then the next that I was recovering. Coupled with all that was the torment of having to watch what his brother Peter was going through with his wife and kids.

Sometimes I wonder if James felt left out or pushed to one side. If he'd felt unappreciated, then I would have understood. I don't think I told him enough at the time how much I loved him – and the same sentiment applies even more so today. It's just another example of me not being a very good father, I'm afraid. All I can say is that when you're in a situation where you don't think you're going to be living for very much longer, as I had recently been, you become a little selfish. Even more selfish than normal, in my case.

Eventually, Peter's family crisis came to a head. The man whose arrival on the scene had caused us all so much grief returned to England, with my ex-daughter-in-law and our grandchildren in tow. We thought that at last there might be some chance of taking him to court (as some of our business arrangements had turned sour, which I could have done without after having gone through my operation and everything else related to it), or of at least achieving visitation rights for Peter with his kids. But it didn't happen. I really felt that Peter's wife didn't want him or us to see the kids. If a mother doesn't want her children to be visited by their father, then she can make things very, very difficult.

Legally, it seemed that Peter, Melinda and I had nowhere to turn as far as obtaining custody of the children went. We hadn't got a leg to stand on. My son's kids – our grandchildren – had been taken, yet we were powerless to get them back.

Hate is a very strong emotion. Lots of people think it's stronger than love. I'm not sure, but hatred is something I reserved for my ex-daughter-in-law's boyfriend, in the light of my son's shattered life and the shattered lives of my grandchildren. For many reasons, I blamed him most of all. How much he cost us emotionally, I can never put a price on. I wanted to hurt this man whose appearance on the scene had caused so much pain to my family – and I wasn't going to stop until I did.

If this man's intention was to destroy me, then the bastard came pretty close. But it was how all this affected my son and Melinda that infuriated me the most. After all my wife had been through during our life together, for her now to have to endure this was intolerable. That was the last straw for me. I got to the stage where all I wanted to do was hurt him.

Those of you with children who are reading this will understand how I felt. Try imagining for a second what it would be like if your son or daughter was taken away from you and you were never able to see them again, your mind being tortured with thoughts of the effect all this might have on your child.

What would you do? If you had it in your power to hit back at the man you saw as responsible for it all, would you do it?

If the law couldn't help, then it seemed to me that someone working outside the law was the only solution. I felt I wanted this man severely dealt with. I wanted him hurt, not just emotionally. Perhaps I even wished him dead. After all, if he was gone, then part of the problem would be gone. Eaten up with anger, I discussed it with Peter.

'Dad, don't be silly,' he said to me. 'Think what would happen if you hired someone and people found out.'

He was right, of course. It seemed that things had come full circle. Now Peter was giving me advice on the situation. He was telling me to behave myself. Nevertheless, I wanted some kind of justice. I still wanted revenge.

One day, I was helping out in the restaurant in Harrogate. A man came up to me, a complete stranger, and said in a very quiet voice, 'I think you may need my help.' He asked me to join him for a coffee, and intimated that there were various methods that could be used to teach this man a lesson. I listened to him and said thank you. He then disappeared.

Believe me, I was tempted – but some temptations are a step too far. Luckily, I made the right choice and walked away. If I could have got my hands on the object of my fury and hatred myself, I would have throttled him. I would have looked at him and watched him take his last gasps of air. That's how much I hated him. I could have gouged his eyes out. I could have nailed him to a plank of wood and shot arrows into him. Yet hate like that is destructive. When you allow that much hate to build up inside you, the only person you damage is yourself.

I now feel very sorry for this man and for my ex-daughter-in-law. I don't want people to think I'm going all religious or gooey, but after all the years of hatred for these people, I now feel nothing but sorrow and contempt for them.

In addition, I know it would have caused my grandchildren even more pain to know that I harboured these thoughts of hatred, from which I have now moved on. They think of this man as a father, after all. He is their mother's husband. If I'd continued to feel that way, I would have hurt them – and I would never do that for anything in the world.

God only knows what kind of influence this man has on their lives now. I have heard that they're both doing very well at school and that's positive. At the end of the day, Peter, Melinda and I console ourselves with the thought that this person and my ex-daughter-in-law will ultimately want good lives for our grandchildren. We hope that one day we will be allowed to meet two well-adjusted young people. I hope so. I want to see them again at some stage and I know my son is desperate to have a proper relationship with them.

Meanwhile, time has passed. Peter is now married again, to a woman who is absolutely amazing. She picked him up and put his life on the straight and narrow again. She has turned him into a completely different person after what he went through. By coincidence, they now live in the same town as Peter's kids and his ex-wife and her husband. Peter sees them in the street sometimes, but he just melts away into the crowd. He doesn't confront them. He stays away, because he loves those children so much.

My son still has all the debts he incurred during that terrible time and he still has the psychological scars – but, thank God, he now has a good future, too.

What I want to make clear to our grandchildren, if they ever read this book, is how much Melinda and I, their dad, his new wife Adele, their half-brother and sister and their Uncle James wanted, and still do want, to be involved in their lives.

In fact, that was one of my reasons for writing this book. I may never see my grandchildren again, but at least if they read this they'll know how much they're loved. How much they've always been loved. The pain and upset that was caused made contact with them impossible, but I want them to realize that we never stopped trying.

If I took anything constructive from this whole wretched experience, it was that Melinda and I learned that we could emerge from another crisis intact. In some strange way, perhaps all that upset happening so soon after my own operation helped to make me stronger. Perhaps it even helped me recover, because it gave me something to focus on.

Life is strange. It's hard and it's difficult to understand at times, but what can any of us do? We're stuck with it.

About fifteen years ago, I was sitting in a restaurant with a producer who worked on my TV show, when a limousine pulled up outside. A tall guy got out, walked into the restaurant and walked straight over to me. It was Luke Goss, one half of the successful eighties pop group, Bros.

'James,' he said, beaming at me and shaking my hand, 'I'm a big fan.'

He's the only celebrity who's ever done that to me. I was delighted.

Maybe six years after that happened, Melinda and I were living in Canary Wharf in London and we bumped into Luke again. It turned out that he and his wife, Shirley, were living nearby. The four of us rapidly became mates. We went out for meals together and became very close.

After my first post-op check-up, not long after the operation on my tumour, Luke rang to ask how I'd got on.

'Great,' I told him. 'I don't have to go back for another three months.'

'Right, we're going out for dinner to celebrate,' Luke told me. 'Let's go to France for dinner tonight.'

Melinda and I only got back from the hospital at four that afternoon, but that didn't matter. We jumped into our car and drove down to Dover. It was a new car: I'd bought myself a soft-top sports car soon after the operation, determined that I was going to have one before I died. There's nothing like putting the top down on the car and feeling the wind on your face as you race along. I'd had those Japanese numbers back in the eighties, but my new motor was the real deal.

We got on the ferry, sailed across the Channel, then drove off at the other side and headed for La Touqet, about half an hour's drive down the coast from Calais. I'd only ever been to Paris and the South of France before on my Gallic travels. Until that evening, I'd never been to northern France. So we came off the ferry full of enthusiasm – and promptly got lost.

There we were, travelling down the motorway in France, me following Luke and him calling on the phone to say: 'I think we've taken the wrong turning.' At least he admitted it – believe me, he's an exceptional man.

We continued driving until we ended up in a little market town called Arras. It was about midnight when we finally drove into the little cobbled square of this town, but there were a couple of restaurants still open. We sat having pizzas at about one in the morning, then drove back, singing the old Bonnie Tyler song 'Lost in France'. It was wonderful.

After that, Melinda and I started going away every weekend. We lived life as fully as we could. I turned fifty in 2001 and, breaking my own rule about celebrating my birthday, I threw a huge bash in honour of making it to the landmark age. Given my health in the run-up to it, I felt lucky to be alive. Melinda and I made the most of every moment – purely and simply because we weren't sure exactly how much life I had left. After the operation, I'd asked the doctor, 'What happens next?'

'I don't know,' he'd told me. 'You could live for two years or you could live for twenty years. I just don't know.'

I had it in my mind that if I got over the two years, I might be okay. So I worked to these time slots, always trying to cram into life as much as I could. I'm still doing that now.

One of the experiences I've managed to squeeze in is appearing in a couple of films. After Luke's music career ended, he went on to become a successful actor. He got me a couple of parts in some of the films he made in this country. He'd already had considerable international success by this time in the vampire film *Blade II* (2002).

One of these British-based movies was *Charlie*, which came out in 2004. It was based on the life of the notorious London gangster of the sixties, Charles Richardson, whom Luke played in the film. The Richardsons were rivals to the Krays in the London underworld and, if anything, they were even more ruthless. Martin and Gary Kemp, brothers who used to be in the band Spandau Ballet, had already played the Kray twins in a film, *The Krays* (1990), so the Richardsons were the next target for British filmmakers. Luke managed to get me a part in the movie. It wasn't exactly a role likely to strike fear into Robert de Niro – I played the part of a man sitting in a bar taking a bribe. Blink and you'll miss me, but I loved it.

After that, Luke went on to star in a horror film called *Cold and Dark* (2005). He got me the part of the main baddie. I didn't have any lines, but I appeared quite a lot in the movie. Melinda and I went down to Cornwall to film this role. I really had a ball. I'd started out as an actor and it now looked as if I was going back to my dramatic roots.

One of the best weekends we ever had was when Luke was actually shooting *Blade II* with Wesley Snipes in Prague. Luke had said to us that we must go over and hang out with him and watch what was happening. So, we went over to Prague. When we got there, we found a message from Luke saying that he couldn't get away because he was filming, but he'd booked us a table in a restaurant on the banks of the Vltava, the river that flows through Prague. It was April so, despite the fact that it was freezing, we sat outside and they brought us huge blankets to keep us warm while we ate. It was a great meal and a great experience.

One night, there was a party for the cast and we were invited. We were picked up in a limousine and taken to this nightclub in a cobbled street in the middle of the city. It looked like the set of a 1950s black-and-white spy movie.

We went into the nightclub, down some stairs and through a door into the cellar, then down again into another cellar and beyond into a third one. It was huge. A massive, cavernous underground room through which music was pumping. The DJ was none other than Wesley Snipes himself. He was playing his records surrounded by a horde of enormous bouncers, even though the only people at the party were actors who'd been in the movie with him. Wesley never left the turntables all night. He just stood there with his headphones on, gyrating around as he played the music.

It reminded me a little of myself when I used to work at Topshop all those years before.

We had a fantastic night. It's one I will never forget. I will always be indebted to Luke and his wife Shirley for picking us up at a time when we were very low. They now live in Hollywood, so we don't see them much, but we still speak on the phone.

That weekend in Prague was just one of the occasions on which Luke showed his generosity towards us. The first Christmas after my operation, Luke hired the penthouse suite of a hotel near us and we had a marvellous celebration. My son Peter, enduring his first Christmas without the kids, also came, and Luke and Shirley went out of their way to ensure he had a good time as well. I'll never forget their kindness to me, Melinda and my whole family. People like Luke are few and far between and I count myself fortunate to know him. Perhaps if he ever makes another film in this country, he can get me a part. Nepotism can be a wonderful thing.

Over the years, as you might expect, I've become friendly with lots of people in the entertainment business, many of whom are now household names. There is something of a misconception among the public that, because I've interviewed or met a lot of huge stars over the years, my phone is constantly ringing with them calling me to say hello or asking me to join them for dinner. It just doesn't work like that. Nonetheless, I've been lucky over the course of my career in meeting many stars and celebrities, and a small number have become my friends.

One of them was the lovely and now sadly departed Bernard Manning. Bernard appeared on many of my radio and TV shows over the years. I know he was not popular with the politically correct brigade, but he was a good-hearted man and, despite the fact that he was more or less ignored by mainstream TV, he had a massive following around the country. He was a very nice guy. All those who condemned him as foulmouthed and racist really didn't know him. There are many better known and better loved celebrities who could have learned a thing or two about charity work from Bernard. I wouldn't hear a word said against him.

A regular caller is Steve Wright. He makes a call to me once a year, just to see if I'm okay, and I really appreciate his concern. Steve is one of radio's genuine talents and he's also a very nice bloke. Getting to know people like him over the past thirty-odd years has really been one of the best parts of what I still consider to be a wonderful job.

Another mate is Dale Winton. I met Dale years ago when he was working on Radio Trent in Leeds and I used to go round to their studios to do voiceovers. Over the course of time, we got chatting.

'I'd love to have a TV show,' Dale said to me one day. 'How did you get yours?'

'Luck,' I told him.

Dale said that was all he wanted to do.

I suggested that if he was more himself he'd probably have more luck. I don't think he wanted to appear to be too camp, because on Radio Trent at that time he had a very butch, deep voice.

We didn't next meet up until a few years later. By then, Dale had secured his own TV show.

'I told you being yourself would work,' I said.

'Yes, you were right, I've done very well,' he told me.

I saw him again at a friend's funeral in Leeds not so long ago. A DJ called Peter Tate had sadly died of brain cancer. He'd been a particular friend of Dale's. After the funeral, Dale said: 'Do you want a lift back to the railway station?'

I did, so off we went. We drove along in Dale's very flash car with the top down, through the middle of Leeds. We stopped at some traffic lights and the person in the vehicle next to us whistled at the car, so Dale fluffed himself up and looked over as if to say hello. Before he could open his mouth, though, the guy driving the other car shouted: 'Oi, James, good to see you back up here in Leeds!'

It made my day.

Later, Dale came on my show at talkSPORT. He and I were in the lift and he said to me: 'James, have you ever considered being gay? You know I've always fancied you. I've always liked you for years.'

'No, I've never considered being gay, Dale,' I told him. 'But if I ever turn, you can be my first conquest.'

In fact, he talked to Melinda on the phone one day, and asked if there was any way they could share me. I was a little shaken when I heard her say that there probably was some kind of arrangement that could be made.

Bless Dale. I could never be gay, but I am very in touch with my feminine side and I get very annoyed at homophobes and people who persecute gay people. Why should people's sex lives bother others so much? Sometimes I wish I was gay, just to piss off all the homophobes out there.

As for Dale, he's a great guy. It's a pity there aren't more straight people like him. The world would be a better place.

Peter Stringfellow, the nightclub owner, is another good friend of mine. I've known Peter for years and he's a fantastic bloke, one of the nicest people I know. I'm aware he's never averse to a little publicity and he's certainly not shy about getting his face in the paper, but one of the things I've always admired about Peter is his single-mindedness. That was one of the reasons he became so successful. He identified a niche in a market and he filled it. That's why his clubs are so popular. He took chances, he followed his hunches and his instincts and he got where he is today through bloody hard work.

He came into his own when I returned to work after my operation. Melinda would take me to the studio every night, then drive me home afterwards. But at that time, wanting to make the most of every single minute I had, once the programme was finished, I didn't always feel like going home. I didn't want to sleep. I wanted to be active. I wanted to fill those empty moments with something. Peter helped me to do that. He made life entertaining for me while I was getting back on my feet. He was always a wonderful host to Melinda and me and I'll always thank him for that.

'Come down to the club when you've finished,' he used to say. 'Come and have a few drinks.'

So, after the show finished at one in the morning, Melinda would drive me to Stringfellows. Fortunately, she loved it too. In fact, I'm sure if she had her time over again she'd become a stripper or pole dancer or model. She's one of the most glamorous people I know and she never had a chance to fulfil that side of her; a chance she should have had. Another thing, I regret to say, for which I must take the blame.

Melinda used to get up and dance with the girls some nights, but one night she got a bit too close to one of the dancers. Peter told me, 'Get her to stop that, James, or we'll have to throw her out. You can't touch my dancers, you know.'

I couldn't see anything wrong with it, but rules are rules, I suppose.

Another night, we were sitting in Stringfellows at about two in the morning, drinking white wine and eating smoked salmon and scrambled eggs, surrounded by half-naked women who were sliding up and down poles. Peter said: 'Since talking to you, James, it's made me realize that none of us live for ever.'

From that point on, he cut down the amount of hours he worked, so that he could enjoy life more. And trust me, if you can't enjoy life surrounded by half-naked women, then you are in trouble.

About twelve years ago, Peter was on the programme talking about something or other. At the end of the show, we were saying our goodbyes.

'You've got to come down to the club tonight,' he told me.

'Why? What are you doing?' I wanted to know.

'We're having a fund-raiser for the Tory Party,' he said. 'If you come down tonight, I'll introduce you to Margaret Thatcher.'

Peter's a staunch Tory and I happen to think that Margaret Thatcher did more for this country than any prime minister for about fifty years, so I readily agreed. I think we have a lot to thank Mrs Thatcher for. I was keen to meet her. Wouldn't anyone be keen to meet a woman who will go down in history?

I turned up at Stringfellows that Sunday night, a little disappointed to see that Peter had given all the dancing girls the night off. I don't think Maggie would have minded, to be honest. The waitresses were all still dressed in their little tutu skirts, though. Not everything in the club had been changed to accommodate this particular set of visitors, I was happy to note.

The club was packed, mostly with fairly stuffy people as you would expect, but Peter managed to alleviate the stuffiness wherever he went. True to his word, he took us to the table next to Margaret Thatcher, where we were duly seated.

It was a really surreal evening. Melinda and I were sitting in Stringfellows next to the country's only female prime minister, while Peter flitted around being the perfect host, as only Peter can.

Mrs Thatcher was almost eighty at that time and her press secretary looked about the same age.

'And what do you do then, dear?' the secretary asked me.

To my delight, Margaret Thatcher suddenly interrupted. 'He's terribly good,' she gushed. 'He's on the radio. Carol likes him.'

I thought this was really nice: a former prime minister of this country telling her own press secretary who I was. I sat there chatting to Margaret Thatcher for twenty minutes. Me, talking to the Iron Lady in a lap-dancing club in the West End. It has to be one of the most bizarre experiences I've ever had.

I'd love to have spoken to her on my programme some time. It wasn't to be.

Another thing we used to do after I'd finished the show was to go to Brick Lane and get a curry. We used to go somewhere most nights. I wanted as much life as I could cram in.

This went on for most of the first year after my operation. I was having check-ups every three months to make sure the cancer hadn't come back.

'When I come in for these appointments,' I said to Tim O'Brien the first time, 'no small talk. Just tell me whether or not things are all right. I don't want any of this "let's have a look at your tests" and all that. I just want to know if I'm all right or if I'm not.'

That's the way Tim did it, and still does it to this day.

I have to go for a check-up just once a year these days. As that date approaches, I still get paranoid. I still feel scared and I know that I get more irritable around people as my appointment draws near. I'm plagued by the twinges and pains that we all get as we get older, but I always think that they're a sign that something's badly wrong again, so I worry fiercely about it until Tim gives me the all-clear once more.

I talk about all this on the air, because there are lots of people going through the same kind of thing that I am. If I can help just one of those people by letting them know they're not alone, then I will consider that worthwhile. Friendship in an hour of need is priceless.

JUST A MOMENT NOW, I'VE GOT SOMETHING TO SAY ...

THE STATE OF BRITISH RADIO

Radio is sometimes viewed as a glamorous business, but I've never found it that way – and I should know. As well as broadcasting for talkSPORT, Radio Aire, BBC Radio Derby and Metro, the stations at which I'm perhaps best known, I've worked at Radio Tees up in the North-East and Century Radio in Newcastle, and I've also plied my trade for BBC Radio London, GLR, LBC, Atlantic 252 and Radio York.

One of the highlights of being around at the beginning of commercial radio is that, in the intervening years, I've seen people make all the mistakes. The sad thing about radio is that people have continued to make the same mistakes. They don't seem to have learned anything. Anything at all.

Radio relies on personalities; it doesn't rely on music choice. It relies on the people on the radio wanting to be on radio; not just using radio as a vehicle to get on to television or some other medium. It needs people who want to work specifically for radio and who have the good of the business at heart. Radio is not the poor relation to TV. Radio can still be one of the most exciting mediums there is. Even with the Internet and computers and all the other technological advances we're seeing, modern radio is still very fresh.

Yet it has to be appreciated for what it is. There are far too many people who go into radio these days to use it as a stepping stone to something else. They want to be big stars on TV, and they think that radio will open the necessary doors. They want it as a stop-gap until something better comes along.

In some ways, though, I can't blame these people. Most radio stations pay their on-air talent crap money. The people who make all the money out of radio are those who go into management. They're the ones who've made enormous amounts of money from the radio industry.

It's definitely not us. Not the DJs. Don't get me wrong, I get paid well, but not the fortune that many people imagine. It's true that household names like Terry Wogan, Chris Tarrant and, nowadays, Chris Moyles make loads of money on radio, but not your average presenter or DJ and certainly not those working for regional stations.

I think the radio industry really needs to appreciate the people who work on its stations. The smaller the station, the more that station has to find its own personalities. It needs to recruit people who are going to stay with the station, and not just wait until they can find a job on a bigger one. All the stations have got to attract some new blood, obviously, but they must also nurture the talents and personalities they already have – if they've got any at all.

Even though I hate doing this kind of thing, I recently spoke at a conference about how personality was dead on radio. Lots of programme directors like to have complete control of their DJs and presenters because they are frightened of personality. They're scared of anything they can't control. Sometimes, they're frightened of originality. That's why the majority of radio is so bland. Most radio stations follow the same tired old formats.

But, ironically, it's personality that listeners want to hear. Let's face it, if you want to hear music, then you use the CD player in your car. There's only one thing that makes a good radio presenter and that's the ability to communicate. Whether you're a DJ playing records or whether you're doing a talk show, that ability should be inherent within you. Lots of people have been doing radio in this country for years and are still deadly dull and boring. They haven't got that natural gift for communication.

In the business these days, there are all too few who do.

I've mentioned in passing two men who have got it: Terry Wogan and Chris Moyles. I think there are two others, both of whom are at talkSPORT like myself: Alan Brazil and Mike Parry. Both came to radio late in their lives, but both have that magic ability. Jason Cundey, a former Chelsea footballer, also has that gift. I'm confident that a lot will be heard from Jason in the future.

There are certain people who've been on the periphery of radio for years and years. They joined the organizations, the clubs. They go to the award ceremonies and they're photographed all over the place. They are the people who control who gets on the air. And, in my opinion, they have absolutely no business getting involved. Radio managers can murder a station's programming – and, it probably goes without saying, I don't think any of them deserve the overinflated salaries they supposedly 'earn'.

I think radio should be reclaimed for the people at the heart of it: the listeners. Give the people what they want. That means originality. That means innovation. That means broadcasters who are committed to the medium. That means personality.

If that happens, then believe me: radio will be around for ever, no matter what the future has in store.

As well as getting back on to the radio after my illness, I also embarked on another adventure in television. I had the need, a year or so after my operation, to get some things out of my system. Perhaps I wanted to prove to myself that I could still do it on TV as well as on the radio.

My latest contribution to the world of television was a series called *The Blue Whale*. My first TV show since *Whale On*, it was made for the satellite channel Men and Motors. I travelled to Manchester to record the whole series and we filmed fifteen one-hour shows in a week. I recorded the TV programmes then did my own talkSPORT broadcast each night from a Manchester studio. I wondered, before this all began, if I was fit enough to do it, but I got through that week so, obviously, I must have been.

The Blue Whale was recorded well in advance, so it didn't have any of the danger attached to a live broadcast, but the format was much the same as the other TV programmes I'd done in the past. It was a pretty off-the-wall show. I wanted a set with a huge fish tank and a woman dressed as a mermaid swimming around in it, but the budget didn't stretch to that, so what we finally had was a charming young lady called Zoe, a glamour model, who sat topless with a fish tail over her legs, looking like a mermaid. There was no swimming pool for her to float around in; instead she sat in a paddling pool for the duration of the show. Every now and then, I'd walk over and spray her with a plant mister. My catchphrase used to be: 'If you're thinking of having a mermaid, you've got to keep her moist.'

It always got a laugh from the crew, but then again, I've always been crass.

The show was shot without the benefit of a studio audience. When you're working without a crowd, you have to rely on the reactions of the crew – especially to gauge the success of any humorous content. The chuckles of the cameramen and sound guys really add to the enjoyment in the studio when you're not working directly to an audience. Presenting to an empty studio doesn't bother me, though. After all, when you're working on radio, the only response you get from your audience is if they start ringing in during a show. Some TV hosts find it impossible to work without an audience to feed off, but I've never found that a problem.

The Blue Whale did remarkably well. Considering we were going out on a satellite channel at one o'clock in the morning, the show still managed to pull in around 250,000 viewers each time it aired.

I think the principle with late-night television is the same as with late-night radio. In short, people are watching at that time because they want to be. Sometimes there might be a guest on whom they particularly want to see interviewed, or they may just like the format of the programme. Who knows, they might even turn on because they like watching me.

I'm sure the attraction of my shows both on radio and television over the years has been the lack of pretence. The only way you can work in broadcasting is to be yourself. Once you start adopting a pretend personality, your audience will see right through you. People watching or listening to me feel that they can speak to me the same way they would speak to someone they lived next door to. I firmly believe that is how talk-radio shows should be conducted. As I've said before, the talk-radio show is the modern-day garden fence. The difference is that, instead of chatting over the garden hedge, anyone who rings in is chatting over the airwaves and millions are listening to their views, instead of just the one neighbour.

The advantage of late-night radio in particular is that, in the darkness of the night, people's minds go off at different tangents. Things they'd never normally have thought about in the brightness of the day can sometimes surface in the stillness of the small hours. Once the sun's gone down, the ensuing blanket of darkness allows you to explore all the wild ideas you wouldn't entertain in the light. It forces you to confront thoughts inside yourself that are best expressed at night. Thoughts you sometimes wish you didn't have. My job as a late-night host is to bring those thoughts out – whether they want to come out or not.

Whichever radio station I've worked on doing the late-night show, I've always kept the studio dark and dimly lit. Usually only the light from the control panels and the monitors breaks through the gloom inside the studio. In most late-night radio stations you go into, the studios are brightly lit. Not mine. The darkness helps me to work better. To be alone, at night, in a darkened radio studio is to allow your mind to wander. It sometimes enables me to venture into areas of discussion perhaps best left in the blackness.

For instance, how much would it take for you to sleep with someone of the same sex?

Ask yourself that question now.

It's a question I might ask on the air if the calls are a little slow. It's one of the questions that's guaranteed to get a response from people, absolutely certain to get them thinking. Most people saw that nineties film with Robert Redford and Demi Moore called *Indecent Proposal* (1993). Just to refresh your memories, it was about a millionaire who offered a woman £1 million if she'd spend the night with him. She took it and had to live with the repercussions afterwards. At the time, the newspapers were full of similar kinds of articles and it got people talking.

Of course, the movie was a cop-out, because in the film the millionaire was played by Robert Redford – hardly the ugliest guy in the world. The choice for many women probably wouldn't have been that hard. Now, if the millionaire had been a humpbacked dwarf, then it might have been a different matter. The choice wouldn't have been so easy.

So, ask yourself my original question again. How much would it take for you to sleep with someone of the same sex? A million pounds? Two million? More?

The purpose of the question isn't to shock or disgust. It's to make people think. It's to get them considering situations they would never normally conceive of themselves and to be so fired up with their own thoughts that they ring in and call my show.

There are probably a dozen other examples I could give you of contentious questions that are guaranteed to provoke some kind of response from listeners. As the host of a talk-radio show, I feel it is my responsibility to make people think, to make them mull over issues they wouldn't usually consider. My question is only the beginning. All kinds of subjects and topics can evolve from one relatively simple question. It's just a matter of coaxing opinions from people.

So, any budding presenters out there, let me tell you, you don't need a university education to work in radio. In fact, I sometimes think that if you spend a long time at university, you just end up working for the BBC, along with some of the other dull and boring people who run radio stations. The only reason these people get so high up is because they've got the right qualifications. They don't have any passion. Academically educated people rarely have any passion. That's why self-made millionaires and entrepreneurs are the best kind of people to be involved with. These people have an idea and carry it through.

The management of talkSPORT is a prime example of entrepreneurial success. In 2004, the station changed owners again, after Kelvin MacKenzie decided to float the company on the Stock Exchange, though he then decided to buy it back himself. However, he couldn't find enough money to buy the station, and it was bought by one of Britain's last independent television companies, Ulster TV. What they brought to the station was more investment. They also had different ideas from ones that would have been presented by another radio company.

What I hope is that, on this printed page, my enthusiasm for radio comes across. It's difficult to explain in words how much I still love it and what it means to me. Radio is a magnificent medium, crammed full of really talented people. Despite the words of that song by The Buggles in the eighties, video never killed the radio star. Nothing will kill the broadcasting talent.

However, the radio industry has to be open to new ideas. For example, talk radio should be huge. At the moment, there's only talkSPORT, LBC and Talk 107 in Edinburgh to cater for people who want to listen to chat on the air. This is ridiculous. We need to have at least a dozen 'speech radio' stations vying for listeners. A nation that is so ready to climb up on soapboxes, write letters of complaint and march in protest against things it doesn't agree with should have more than just three talk-radio stations on which to vent its views. Too many people have too much to say for this situation to continue. There are too many worthwhile opinions out there for them to be confined to just three stations.

And I say to all radio stations, if somebody doesn't like what you broadcast, then they don't have to fucking listen. They can turn the bloody radio off. Particularly when I'm on. Because why should any talk-radio host have to worry about offending people? If people were that offended by what we did, we wouldn't be there, because the listeners wouldn't listen. It's that simple.

If you've got a viewpoint to put across, then you should never be afraid of expressing it, and that's what I've always done. I say contentious things, I say provocative things and many people think I say them only to be deliberately controversial, but this isn't the case. The views I express on my radio show are views that I genuinely hold. They're not always popular with people, but if that's the case, then I'm afraid it's tough luck.

For example, I think handguns are very sexy. They've had a very bad press since the terrible events at Hungerford and Dunblane, and I must admit, until I fired one, I didn't realize what magnificent things they were. I was lucky enough to shoot some handguns during my trip to Chicago back in the eighties. Of course, the police there carry guns all the time. Even off duty, my friend Mike carried two guns: one in a shoulder holster under his left arm, and another in an ankle holster. We were having a drink one night when I spotted his revolver in the ankle holster. The butt was poking out of the top of his cowboy boot.

'I can see your gun,' I told him, a little bit unsettled by the fact that I was so close to a firearm.

'Don't worry about it,' Mike said.

'Why are you carrying a gun when you're off duty?' I persisted.

'Jamie, baby,' he said, smiling. 'You are a guest in the great metropolis of Chicago. How do you think I'd feel if you were to get shot while you were here as my guest?'

I didn't know how he'd feel, but I certainly didn't want to find out.

It was after that discussion about guns that Mike told me I should see some up close; fire some. The following day, he, Graham Pollard and I went down into the basement of the precinct house to the firing range there, and I fired guns for the first time in my life.

It was a great experience. As I said before, there's something very sexy about holding that piece of polished cold steel and knowing that you're about to fire a bullet from it that will travel through the air at over one thousand feet a second.

You grip the wooden butt of the gun, you aim at the man-shaped target, squinting down the sights, and you squeeze the trigger. You have to wear ear protectors because the sound would deafen you. That's one of the things that they never seem to portray accurately in films: the deafening blast that accompanies every shot from a gun. I've spoken to a mate of mine who used to fire guns for a hobby and he agrees. What you see on the big screen is nothing like the reality when you fire a handgun.

Nothing prepares you for the massive recoil, either. When you squeeze that trigger, you're not expecting the gun – and your whole arm – to fly upwards. It's impossible to prepare yourself for that initial jolt.

We spent the whole morning in that firing range, blasting away at targets under Mike's watchful eye. Graham got on particularly well at target shooting and announced that he must be a natural shot. However, Mike told us that most people hit the bull's-eye on their first attempt because they are being extra careful, and because they're being guided by an instructor. It's only when they become more confident with a gun – and less afraid of it – that they get a little complacent. When that happens, their aim usually goes slightly off.

Shooting takes a tremendous amount of self-discipline and concentration. It was something I always thought I'd have liked to have taken up. Perhaps it would have been the natural progression from my teenage archery. That also had the need for practice, discipline and concentration, if you wanted to be good at it. Unfortunately, I never got the chance to take up pistol shooting when I came back to this country, but I will always be grateful to Mike for giving me the chance to experience what it's like to hold such incredible weapons in my hand.

Something Mike told me on many occasions has also stuck with me: it isn't guns that kill people, it's people who kill people. The tragedies at Dunblane and Hungerford were down to Thomas Hamilton and Michael Ryan, the men who pulled the triggers – not the people who manufactured the guns they used, and not the people who went about their business lawfully week in and week out at gun clubs all around this country. The fact that gun crime has increased in this nation since all legal handguns were banned would seem to support the argument that banning them was a knee-jerk reaction. It isn't legally owned weapons that kill people in this country; it's those that are bought so easily illegally.

To be a supporter of guns or even of the right to own them isn't a popular stance these days, but then again, being in a minority when it comes to a particular viewpoint has never bothered me. If it had, you wouldn't be reading this book now.

Derek Acorah is a medium and he's been on my radio show many times. Usually when he appears, he upsets lots of people, because many listeners don't believe in the hereafter and they think Derek's a bit of a charlatan. But whatever people say about him, first and foremost, Derek is entertaining. Whenever he's on, we get hundreds of calls from people wanting to talk to him. Many believe that he's in contact with 'the other side' and they find that fascinating. With Derek comes Sam, his spirit guide. When I get fed up with talking to Derek, I interview Sam.

I've had other mediums on and they've complained that the conditions aren't right for them, that the atmosphere isn't conducive to contacting the spirits or stuff like that. Not Derek. People ring up to find out what their departed loved ones are up to in the great beyond and Derek never fails to have some sort of contact. I think the main thing is that the people who have rung in asking Derek for information are left feeling, hopefully, a little bit comforted. I think we're all desperate to know if there is anything to look forward to beyond death, and people like Derek can be of great solace to some grieving people.

When I was in hospital, not long after my operation, the phone rang at about nine o'clock one evening. It was dark inside the ward. I was lying there connected to machines by tubes and the phone was brought to me. It was Derek. He seemed slightly inebriated at the other end of the line, almost in tears, but then I was full of morphine at the time.

'James,' he wailed. 'I don't know what to say.'

'What's wrong, Derek?' I asked, thinking he'd had a few too many.

'I knew you were going to get cancer and I didn't tell you anything,' he told me.

'Really?' I thought.

'But I knew you were going to be all right,' he added.

As long as he knew, that's fine then, isn't it?

Perhaps he did know. I'll never know the truth.

Derek still comes on the show. Whether what he says about 'the other side' and life after death is true or not, I can only imagine. Personally, I don't want to find out the truth for many years to come. About thirty years ago, I experienced what could be described as a near-death incident, or at least what felt like a near-death, out-of-body experience, and that was plenty close enough for me. Despite the time lapse, I can remember it as if it took place yesterday.

Melinda and I were living in Prudhoe at the time; I was working on Metro Radio. I had to go to the dentist for a filling one day. He was using gas instead of the injections that are commonplace these days. So, he gave me the gas and I lay back in the dentist's chair, blissfully unaware of all the drilling and filling that was about to take place. What happened next, I cannot explain to this day.

I banged my head on the surgery ceiling.

The impact seemed to rouse me a little and I looked down to see myself sitting in the dentist's chair. I tried to gather my thoughts. I was feeling claustrophobic and couldn't move my head back because it was wedged against the ceiling. I was watching my own body seated in the chair below – the same body that, a moment later, got up and shook hands with the dentist. I then began to walk towards the door.

At that point, I started panicking. I thought I was going to be stuck in the corner of that room for the rest of my life. I had no idea what would happen if my body walked out of the dentist's surgery. I made a huge mental effort to get back inside my physical self. It was like a jump. A leap back into my own body.

I came to on the floor of the surgery, with the dentist and his nurse in fits of hysterical laughter.

'What are you laughing at?' I asked, blankly.

'I think you were having a dream,' the dentist told me.

To this day, I don't think it was a dream. I think my spirit had left my body and I'd endured an out-of-body experience. I'm sure Derek Acorah would have been able to explain it.

That particular incident alone is one of the reasons that I've always been drawn to having weird guests on my night-time show. Speaking of guests, there are certain people whom I have on the show quite regularly, either because I enjoy talking to them, or because they provoke such a good response from the listeners. Someone who provoked such a response wasn't on the show in the flesh, as such. She was an American porn star called Trixie Q.

A couple of years ago, our programme used to have a link to her website. On it, you could see her doing exercises and aerobics via a webcam. People would log on to the site and watch Trixie doing her exercises, getting all sweaty and gyrating along to the accompanying music. When she'd finished doing her routine, she used to talk to me and it was very amusing. The real twist then came. She used to sell off her sweaty underwear and exercise clothes to the highest bidder. People who had just been watching her on their webcams could become the proud owners of her soggy leotards.

I thought it was a great idea. I always wondered if she vacuum-packed the items to keep them fresh.

Another guest who's been on the show a few times is David Icke, the British writer and public speaker. I think too many people are too quick to dismiss David as a nutcase. Just because he once said that he thought he was Jesus, I don't see why he should be looked on as a figure of fun. If you listen to him carefully (and you have to, because he talks very quickly), he makes a lot of sense. I believe that he's beginning to be taken more seriously. I'm not saying he's right about everything – it takes a lot for me to believe in shape-shifting lizard people – but there are some things he's hit upon that strike a chord.

Guests who have strong views on some of the conspiracy theories that the Internet and newspapers love so much are usually good value as well. The supposed suicide of Dr David Kelly always prompts a provocative discussion on the show. Whether this government scientist was murdered by MI6 or took his own life seems to fascinate listeners – and will do for years to come. Any new information about this case, and anyone with anything to say about it, are guaranteed to provoke the sort of debate that I enjoy so much on my programme.

I'm never interested in having someone on my show who's there solely to promote a new film, album or book. If that film, album or book is interesting and the person plugging it has something worthwhile to say, then that's fair enough, but to be honest, most of the writers I've interviewed have been appallingly dull people who exist only inside their own heads. Many actors are only good value when they're being fed lines to respond to; many rock stars are incoherent anyway. If anyone has a film, album or book to promote and they want their ego massaged, then they should go on TV. I want guests who have something to say that's worth hearing, who have opinions and who will provoke discussion. And, to be honest, the guests usually have to be prepared to take a backseat, because once the audience starts ringing in and asking questions, then I'm more interested in the views of the public.

Some guests turn up with no idea of what my interview technique is like (some would say it isn't really a technique). I always think that any guest going on any show should have some knowledge of the format of that show before they appear. Not to research that is just sheer laziness.

For the most part, I want guests who are going to engender some kind of reaction – firstly with me, but also with my listeners. Politicians are usually good in that respect, but it's difficult to get them to come into the studio. With the show being live, they can't always have their well-rehearsed answers prepared, and God forbid a member of the public might ask them a question that they can't answer as well as they would like.

I think that's why live radio is so much more preferable to pre-recorded material. You get to see how well people respond when they're put on the spot. You hear if someone actually has the ability to use their wits and think on their feet. Recorded interviews are a waste of time.

I recently interviewed David Cameron. I think he's a plonker. He wouldn't come on the programme live and he insisted that the interview be recorded. I asked him why.

'I'm a family man,' he told me. 'I've got children to look after, so I need to be home at night.'

Pathetic. The contempt that man has for ordinary people is beyond belief. In the end, I relented and he came into the studio and I recorded an interview with him. It was barely worth it. He was the most uninspiring man I've ever had the misfortune of meeting. If, at the time you're reading this book, he is the prime minister of this country, then I think we're all doomed. Having said that, I am one of the biggest critics of Tony Blair and the appalling way he mismanaged Britain.

Frankly, I think politicians are all much of a muchness. It's just that when you get them alone in a darkened studio, facing questions they're unprepared for, at least you get to see the ones who deserve their overinflated salaries – and trust me, there are very few who do.

Other guests I invite on the show simply because I want to have them on the programme. They might be people I particularly want to meet. I recently interviewed Sean Bean for exactly that reason.

A guest I've had on the show a number of times is Uri Geller. People say to me: 'Why do you have him on? He's a fake.' I don't believe he is a fake. I don't know what he does or how he achieves it, but I sat in the studio one night watching a spoon bend before my eyes. Not a spoon held in his hand or in my hand, but one that had been placed on the desk in front of me. No one touched that spoon, and yet the metal bent as I watched it. I have no idea how it happened. I have never seen anyone else be able to bend anything without touching it. If there's anyone reading this who can, then please get in touch. I'd like to know how it's done.

Uri's great, and so are his family. He can be a little intense at times, but who cares?

When Uri renewed his wedding vows back in March 2001, he very kindly invited Melinda and me to the ceremony. One of the big celebrity magazines like *Hello!* or *OK!* was covering it. His best man was going to be his then best friend, none other than Michael Jackson.

Melinda and I duly turned up at the special event, feeling completely out of place among all the megastar celebrities who were in attendance. We were seated next to the singer Justin Hayward, from the Moody Blues, and his wife Marie. I knew Justin because he'd been on my show a few times and also because I'd met him back in the seventies when I was working in Newcastle and he was doing a promotional tour for an album. We sat there chatting, waiting for Uri's famed best man to arrive.

Now, I've heard of waiting for the bride to arrive, but at this service, it was completely different. We all sat there, the whole congregation, waiting for the best man.

Michael Jackson finally turned up, approximately two hours late. He spoke to a few people, and he actually asked to speak to Justin Hayward.

'Be careful, Justin,' I said. 'He might ask to buy your entire back catalogue.'

Justin was really excited and that struck me as a little bizarre. Justin Hayward himself is something of a musical legend, with hits like 'Knights in White Satin' and 'Forever Autumn' – and yet there he was like a star-struck teenager, jumping up and down at the possibility of meeting Michael Jackson. I found it quite surreal.

I actually met Michael Jackson myself a year later at, of all places, Exeter City Football Club. Uri had bought a controlling interest in the club and he asked me to act as a compere when Michael Jackson made an appearance there. Melinda and I duly travelled down and watched the match. Michael Jackson came along and I was introduced to him.

I remember shaking hands with him. He had a very delicate, almost limp handshake. He is very fragile. Upon seeing him at Uri's special event, I'd thought: 'This man needs some friends.' Up close, I could see that his face was caked in make-up to hide his scars and sores. His fingernails were a yellowish colour and looked as if they were about to fall off.

'How are you? Very pleased to meet you,' he said. That was about it.

I was going to tell him that, many years ago, when I was working at Radio Aire, I'd introduced him at Roundhay Park in Leeds at a huge festival he played, but I never got the chance. Michael's fellow superstar

Madonna once played that same venue back in those days, and I introduced her, too. Strange as it may sound (or not), she never turned up at Exeter City Football Club.

Speaking of Michael Jackson and Madonna, let's not forget that my career in radio began as a DJ, in charge of the turntables at Topshop and several hot London clubs. Despite the fact that I work in talk radio now, throughout my career I've played music on my shows. I've always loved music. In fact, it's what attracted me to being a DJ in the first place. Over the years, there have been some great musicians whose work I've played on my programmes, who've appeared on my shows, and whom I've been fortunate enough to get to know.

Peter Straker, whom I first met in Newcastle, has got such an unusual and amazing voice. He used to come on my programme and we became firm friends. He was also, at one time, a friend of Queen's lead singer, Freddie Mercury.

The musician Jim Diamond appeared on a number of my TV shows and Melinda and I have become very friendly with Jim and his wife, Chris. Someone once described Jim as Britain's best white soul singer. He has got the most incredible voice. He wrote and sang the theme tune to the TV series *Boon*, which starred Michael Elphick. He was also in a group called PhD, who were very successful in the eighties. 'I Should Have Known Better' was one of his big hits. He's a lovely guy. Occasionally dour, but then again, he is a Scotsman.

Andy Fairweather-Low played a set on my show recently. Andy used to be part of the group known as Amen Corner, who were huge in the sixties and seventies.

Not many people on commercial radio get singers to perform live on their programmes. I've always done it. I know that the people I've mentioned aren't in the same league as Madonna and Michael Jackson, or even any of the one-hit wonders who clog our airwaves these days, but they're all genuinely talented people who've been doing what they do for thirty or forty years. To me, that's the sign of true talent. Longevity.

True talent isn't signalled by how many of your first and only album you can sell. It isn't measured by how many teenyboppers are outside the venue when you leave, waving copies of *Top of the Pops* magazine at you. It certainly isn't judged by how many votes you got on the talent show you won.

A sign of true talent is that you can sing and write and perform music to audiences and record-buyers year in, year out. The people I've mentioned, and many like them, have done that and continue to do it to this day. They might not be on Radio 1's playlist. They might not be top of the download charts or have MTV salivating over their newest state-of-the-art video, but they have a hardcore of fans, many of whom have been with them from the beginning, and will always be there for them.

The same applies in many fields, not just music. Truly talented people just go about their business without courting the limelight and expecting adulation. They do it for the love of their business – just like I've done with radio.

People sometimes say to me: 'It must be terrible not doing TV all the time.' Well, it isn't, I can assure you. I do pop up on television every now and then, but radio is and always will be my first love. There's a connection with listeners that you don't get with viewers when you're on TV. There's an intimacy about radio that television can never capture. When I spent two years solid doing TV, I missed the continuity that came from doing a radio show every night.

The most perceptive critics of radio are your own listeners, and I'm happy to say that I have some of the most wonderful listeners around. I trust that I'm doing them justice with my shows. I truly feel that talkSPORT itself is on the strongest footing ever. In fact, the station's just won the prestigious Gold Award at the 2007 Arqiva Commercial Radio Awards. In addition, we scooped the Station of the Year Award. Guess we must be doing something right, and I think the listeners agree.

A RANT ON REPRODUCTION

If you want my view on what we should do about the juvenile delinquency that terrorizes this country at the moment, it's dead simple.

Nobody should be allowed to breed unless they have a licence.

Under my plans, every baby boy would be sterilized at birth and the operation could then be reversed if he wanted to breed. However, it would be reversed only if he could prove that he was fit to bring a new human being into the world. There would be a set of strict criteria that would have to be met:

Does he have enough money?

Can he house a new member of the human race?

Does he intend to remain with the mother of the child?

If all these questions were answered correctly (i.e. 'yes' to all three), then he would be allowed to have the operation reversed and he would then be permitted to breed. People should not be allowed to reproduce without passing certain tests.

Mind you, under these criteria, I would never have been allowed to reproduce, but that's another story.

I also think laws should be brought in to the effect that

if you have more than two children, you are behaving in an anti-social way and you can be heavily penalized through tax. Two children are enough for anyone.

Both these measures would breed out the inadequate human beings that we decent people have to run the gauntlet of every Friday and Saturday night while going about our lawful business. I'm sick of seeing gangs of hooded morons sloping around like refugees from *Planet of the Apes*, texting each other on stolen phones and listening to music on iPods they've just pinched from hard-working people. Over the last ten or twenty years, society has been plagued by a lack of discipline and a lack of standards. We are a chav nation in many respects – and that applies to all classes of society. The upper classes are as much to blame for the welter of useless individuals as the working classes. The only difference is that the upper classes mainly shag one another, so their particular gene pool doesn't expand too alarmingly.

Breed out the inadequates.

Something else that would help this plan would be to castrate anyone who is imprisoned. Cut their bollocks off!

Criminals should never be allowed to breed again. I don't see why my hard-earned taxes should be lavished on people who are merely a burden on society. After all, most kids learn their behaviour from watching their parents. What kinds of behaviour are the children of criminals going to learn? How best to nick stuff from the local supermarket? How they can hot-wire a car efficiently?

I say, lock the criminals up and castrate them. Breed out the inadequates.

It's the only hope our nation has.

Charity. It's a word that's linked all too readily with celebrities sometimes. People are impressed that well-known people are doing their bit for needy causes, be it an AIDS charity dinner in Hollywood, where the attendees are paying $5,000 for their dinner, or the latest Red Nose Day when, in pursuit of public money and not a little publicity, figures from the entertainment industry can be seen with African children.

It has always irritated me slightly that people who earn such vast amounts of money are constantly on TV asking ordinary people to part with theirs for worthy causes. If each of these so-called celebrities contributed a mere third of their yearly salaries, then we could clear the Third World debt, never mind just building a few wells in Africa.

When I left hospital back in 2000, enormously beholden to Tim O'Brien, the man I felt had saved my life, I was determined to do something positive to help others who had suffered, and would suffer, from the same kind of cancer that I had had.

'What do you need, Tim?' I had asked him.

'We need money for research and we also need to spend money to make people aware of kidney cancer,' he'd informed me. 'It's not a cancer that people know a lot about.'

With everything else that happened immediately after I came out of hospital, it wasn't until five or six years after the operation that I finally got around to starting my charity, which I called the James Whale Fund for Kidney Cancer. It's a type of cancer that seems to be becoming more prevalent, so I wanted to help in as many ways as possible.

I got a few people on board, but it was difficult. Nick Owen, who has suffered from kidney cancer himself, was great, and so too was Pete Waterman, but no one really wants to give money to charity any more. That's how it seems. I'm chairman of the Heritage Foundation this year so, hopefully, my increased profile in that office may help my own fund-raising efforts. The Heritage Foundation is the organization which goes around slapping those blue discs on houses where famous people were born. Being their president means I have to go to the kinds of functions I normally try to keep clear of, but it's a small price to pay and they're good people.

I want to be able to raise enough money for my charity to enable it to give out a couple of grants a year to people doing research into kidney cancer. Two drug companies have developed a drug that helps people with the disease. The drug helps to prolong patients' lives if they're very ill. It seems to me that everyone who needs that drug should have it, but, unfortunately, that isn't what happens at the moment. The NHS is being very slow in making this drug available to those who need it. Many patients don't even know it exists.

My charity was officially launched in September 2006. It has a website, www.jameswhalefund.org, and is run by, amongst others, a man called Nick Turkentine, who is doing a great job with no money. Or should I say, not enough money. It's not such a problem getting members of the public to give cash, but it's incredibly hard getting companies or the government to help.

Raising awareness is the most important aspect of what we do. I feel that is part of my duty having had this disease. The James Whale Fund for Kidney Cancer exists for this purpose. The website is there so that people suffering from the disease can exchange stories with others who have had it or are going through treatment. Basically, people who are or have been in the same boat. When I told everyone on my radio show that I had cancer, the thing that helped me more than anything else was the enormous amount of people who got in touch to tell me that they'd had the same kind of cancer and recovered. That's the reason the charity is there: to provide a similar forum for support, advice and understanding. If I can help just one person with this disease to cope, then I will feel that everything's been worthwhile.

I keep threatening to write to one hundred of the well-known people I've come across in my time, saying: 'Send me a hundred quid and I won't ask you to attend a charity ball and I won't ask you to send me any of your old ties.' I'm sure they'll fall over themselves to do it. If they don't, I'll simply go round to their houses and show them my scar.

An advantage of being a recognizable broadcaster, aside from the noble benefit of being able to raise awareness of issues like kidney cancer, is that you sometimes get things for nothing. Believe me, it doesn't happen to me very often.

A mate of mine, who's a writer, once told me that he always used to mention Wrangler jeans and Puma trainers in the acknowledgements of his novels, in the hope that he'd get some freebies. If it worked, he said, he'd start mentioning that every novel was written in the backseat of a Ferrari, while he quaffed Dom Pérignon champagne.

I think the most he ever got was some free typing paper.

I know some manufacturers, restaurants and shops are only too happy to shower well-known faces with freebies, but in my case I've only ever received a few free suits from tailors in Leeds when I was doing *The James Whale Radio Show*. I had a penchant for waistcoats back in those days ... but that's another story.

One of my passions is Indian food and, I'm delighted to say, to this day I still get my fair share of free meals in Indian restaurants around the country. The beauty of having had TV shows that went out late at night is that practically every Indian restaurant in the country knows who I am when I go in. I have an enormously faithful audience of British Asians. Some people think that because of my outspoken views on stuff like multiculturalism, I'm against people from other countries and cultures, but, of course, that isn't the case. We live in a country made up of people from other parts of the world. We are a country of mongrels. It's one of the best things about our nation.

I'm a mongrel myself, as I've said before. Fortunately, they allow mongrels like me into Indian restaurants. Thirty-odd years ago, I became hooked on Indian food. I love it. Wherever I am in the country, whatever I'm doing, I have to seek out an Indian restaurant. I have

many favourites among them, but the one that stands out
in my mind is a restaurant owned by a man called Enan
Ali. It's called La Raj and it's situated near the Epsom
Downs, about three-quarters of a mile from the very spot
where I was born. Of course, back in the fifties there was
no such thing as Indian restaurants. There were no
Chinese takeaways either, or pizzerias for that matter. All
there was in the days of my youth, as far as takeaway
food was concerned, was fish and chips.

I first met Enan Ali about fifteen years ago, when I
was doing a daytime show for the BBC called *What's the
Job?* Each week I went out and tried to get a job that
wouldn't normally be brought to prominence. It's an idea
that's been repeated many times since, but I did one of
the first series. One week I became a monk. I particularly
enjoyed that. Every monk reminded me of Elton John for
some reason. Another week I was an AA patrolman. I
didn't like that so much, I must admit. A third
programme saw me become a chef in an Indian
restaurant, mainly because I'd told the producers how
much I liked Indian food.

At that time, Enan used to arrange pleasure flights
over London, then take everyone back to his restaurant
for a curry. This, combined with the growing reputation
of his restaurant, was making him something of a
celebrity himself. Enan's restaurant is a bit off the
beaten track, but because of his talent for self-
promotion, he's had all sorts of people in his
establishment. The walls of his high-street emporium
are covered with photos of himself with some of the
famous people who've eaten there, in much the same
way as some American diners decorate their walls with
pictures of famous patrons.

So, as part of the BBC programme, I went to his restaurant and was filmed being a chef for a day in La Raj. I think it was an even bigger thrill for me because the restaurant was so close to where I was born. It was as if I was coming home. It was a great experience. Enan and I have stayed in touch ever since.

Enan organizes the Curry Awards, an annual contest in which he judges, quite simply, the best curries of the year. I was lucky enough to attend the most recent of these events. It was the most fantastically arranged extravaganza, mercifully without the usual horde of celebrities anxious to be spotted at something like this. The only drawback was that I caught a glimpse of Ulrika Jonsson, but even that wasn't enough to put me off.

The food was out of this world. Restaurants from all over the British Isles entered. There were lots of different categories, including awards for the best takeaway curry and the best supermarket curry. It was an evening of indulgence for those of us who love Indian cuisine.

I must admit, I think it's almost impossible to find bad Indian food around the country now. I wish I could mention every single restaurant I've ever enjoyed a meal in, but there have been so many. Who knows? Perhaps if talkSPORT get fed up with me and sack me, I can go back to cooking Indian food full-time. I only did it for one day, but I reckon I'd be a pretty good chef.

The only danger is I might eat all the food before it got to the customers.

'Good evening and welcome to *The James Whale Show*. This is me, the mayor of London, speaking to you.'

If I'd had my way, and the voters had supported me in the numbers I think they might have, that's the sort of introduction you could have been hearing on my programme every night.

Over the years on my radio and TV shows, I've interviewed politicians and I've taken them to task on many occasions, but the idea of actually being a politician myself was something that hadn't struck me.

Not until it was suggested to me by someone else.

In October 2006, I invited Nigel Farage into the studio to talk about the European Parliament. Nigel's the leader of UKIP, the UK Independence Party. I have an enormous amount of respect for him. He believes, as I do, that when Britain joined the EU, we should not have given away so much power to a bunch of faceless bureaucrats, who sit in Brussels making decisions about whether our cucumbers should be straight, or our bananas should curve at a certain angle ... as well as determining the fate of many other, much more significant issues. The fact that these people are unelected is even worse. They sit there making decisions that affect us all, and yet not one of them has any kind of mandate from the people in the first place. No one knows who they are. No one wanted them there, but we are all affected by their decisions in some way, shape or form.

These pillocks in Brussels have deemed it impossible for us to move around from country to country in Europe without a crippling amount of red tape. I personally believe that we should be able to move anywhere in the world and set up home, if we can afford to. People should be allowed to go anywhere they want to, as long as they contribute and don't become a drain on the economy of that particular country.

The people that we elect to the European Parliament can talk until they're blue in the face, and usually do, but, ultimately, the power rests with the European Commissioners. These faceless bureaucrats are the ones with the real power – and they are not elected. We don't know who they are or what their backgrounds are. One of the few we do know about is Neil Kinnock. He became a European Commissioner, discovered for himself a second career and seemingly underwent a radical change of political views.

Living with our European neighbours in peace is a good thing, but handing some of our sovereignty to them is another matter. It isn't xenophobic to argue against this, not on my part and certainly not on the part of Nigel Farage, because he's married to a German lady. It's a matter of losing our rights and our power. In addition, there seems to be so much corruption within this organization that it's worrying. We have to be careful.

Nigel and I talked about these issues on the show.

Nigel speaks from the heart and he's prepared to listen and talk without worrying about what he's saying, which is probably not a good idea for a politician, but it's something I appreciate.

'You should become a candidate for mayor of London,' Nigel told me.

I had never considered this before he asked me, but then I decided I'd do it.

'How difficult could it be,' I thought, 'being in charge of one of the greatest cities in the world?' And having your own radio show. I could actually administer my mayorship from behind the microphone.

The activities of the mayor of London don't just affect the people who live in the city itself. With London being the capital of this country, what goes on within it affects people all over the land. Especially when they drive into the city centre and discover they've got to pay a congestion charge.

I began to think more and more seriously about the possibility of becoming mayor of London. I honestly thought that if there was an election, I might well triumph.

I did a number of interviews with the media during this time. On the way to an appointment at ITN, Melinda turned to me in the back of the car and said: 'You know there is a danger you could win this.'

'That'd be a turn up for the books, wouldn't it?' I replied.

But somewhere at the back of my mind was the belief that I could win, that I could become the mayor of London. This wasn't a power trip for me. It wasn't a desire to become the kind of person I'd interviewed for so many years, the kind of person I'd vilified so often on my show. I wanted the position out of genuine concern for the people of London. I felt that I was more in touch with normal people than the average politician, many of whom have been to private schools and led privileged lives in upper-class surroundings. I was one of the common men. I understood people.

How difficult could it be? The job of a politician is to communicate. He's supposed to communicate the hopes and desires of the common man to others in Parliament. My whole life has been spent communicating. I felt I was qualified.

Unfortunately, Ofcom, that august body that seems to exist for no apparent reason, that official regulator of what is broadcast on both TV and radio, told me I couldn't do it.

'I hope James is joking,' they told talkSPORT. 'You can't be a candidate for any sort of political party in an election and be on the air as well.'

I thought those sorts of rules didn't apply any more. After all, George Galloway, a representative of the Respect Party, has his own regular show on talkSPORT.

Apparently, rules are made not to be broken, but to be twisted accordingly.

It was a choice then between going into politics or remaining on the air.

I had no choice. I couldn't afford not to work, so my aspirations to become mayor of London had to be shelved.

However, if I'd been ten or fifteen years younger, it might have been a different story. I think you need to be in your mid-twenties or your thirties to begin a career in politics. Most of the pillocks who inhabit the House of Commons are around that age when they start. I'm sure most politicians set out with very noble aims; it's only as they get older and more corrupt that their principles are jettisoned.

Perhaps in years to come, I might again consider standing for the post of mayor of London. So many people ring in to my show to tell me that I should be in politics. As I said before, I'm confident I could win a vote if one came about. If the secret of being a good politician is being able to connect with people and get one's message across, then I feel I am better qualified than most of those doing the job now. After all, it's what I've been excelling at on the radio for the past three decades.

The only thing that might hold me back is a quality that has always been a major asset in my career as a broadcaster: I'm honest. Honesty and politics don't make very good bedfellows.

Or is that just me being cynical again?

The difficult thing about writing this book wasn't penning the beginning or the middle – it was trying to come up with a suitable ending. If I'd been writing it seven or eight years ago, there was every chance it could have ended with my premature death. Back then, it seemed that my illness was going to cut short my broadcasting career for good. Luckily (although there are probably several thousand people out there who would dispute that), I survived. I'm still here – and I plan to be around for a long time to come.

Something I discovered during the writing process was that doing an autobiography isn't the great cathartic process I'd expected. It's a pain in the arse. You forget things. You forget names and dates and it's difficult trying to remember them. Also, anyone reading this who's about to start writing their own autobiography, novel, non-fiction book or kids' story, be prepared to be interrupted by the fucking phone every five minutes. I've never known my phone to ring so much as it did while I was attempting to write this book.

I don't know what the future holds. There are lots of things I'd like to do, but to be honest, just getting up every day is a bonus. In terms of my industry, the future is probably going to be people broadcasting online. I could see myself as an affiliate of U. T. V. Radio, broadcasting on the net; on Whale Wireless. I can see it now. W-H-A-L-E. That would be my call sign.

I'd like to continue in radio; I'd like to work in TV again: both for a good few years to come. I think, or rather hope, that I still sound as if I'm enjoying myself when I'm broadcasting. I love my job. When I stop loving it, I'll finish.

When I was a kid, I used to dream of being a cowboy, of being John Wayne. Perhaps that's what I should do. Hit the road. Set up my own mobile radio station in the back of a car. I'd pack all the equipment into it, invite Melinda along, and then I could drive around broadcasting from a different location every night.

It would have to be at night. I've spent most of my working life plying my trade during the small hours.

As each new day dawned, we'd cruise around, stopping here and there for an Indian meal, then, as night approached once more, I'd prepare for the next show. The sun would be sinking. It would be time to go to work. Time for me to drive off into the sunset, just like John Wayne.

The Duke and I have a few things in common. He had cancer, too. He was always honest and he said what he thought, without caring what people thought of him.

The only difference is, I don't think John Wayne ever had an argument with anyone about global warming.

NOT SO FREE SPEECH

When I completed my autobiography I looked proudly at the manuscript and thought, 'That's that.'

A mate of mine who happens to be a writer once told me that the best parts about writing a book were typing the title page and hitting the last full stop; it was just the words in the middle that wore a bit of a pain. I can empathize with that. I didn't expect to be adding an extra chapter just for inclusion in the paperback edition. I certainly didn't expect that extra chapter to be about my dismissal from talkSPORT.

When the first draft of the manuscript was finished (yes, I know it might be hard to believe but there was more than one), as far as I was concerned, I'd told my story. There was nothing else to say. I was pretty much where I wanted to be in life. Naturally, there were still other goals and ambitions I had but, for the most part, I was happy with my lot and relatively at ease with myself. I couldn't have begun to suspect what was lying in wait for me.

These latest developments started at the beginning of 2008. Melinda and I were on holiday in Normandy in France and we'd been having, just in case you care, a lovely time. We were sitting at a restaurant called The Mermaid, overlooking the sea, when my mobile rang. It was Moz Dee, the new programme director at talkSPORT. Moz had been a presenter on the station about ten years earlier and I knew him pretty well. He was a smartly dressed man, invariably clad in a jacket and tie. We'd always got on and I'd never had any problems with him. Only weeks earlier he'd taken me out for dinner in London and outlined his plans for the station, telling me personally how important I was to talkSPORT. The fact that I'd won the UTV award for Current Affairs Presenter of the Year had impressed Moz and quite a few other people at the station as well. They can't have thought I was that bad, can they? Moz had told me that there was to be a new digital talk channel opening and that I'd be very much involved in that. Everything seemed fine. We discussed the format and the content of my programme and Moz respected the fact that I would continue to broadcast in the way that had earned me so many listeners over the years. So I had no reason to be wary of a call from Moz a few weeks later.

It was busy inside the restaurant so I nipped outside to answer the phone, feeling relaxed and without a care in the world. Moz informed me that there had been a complaint about something I'd said on my show in the run-up to the London Mayoral elections, in which I had allegedly shown a preference to one candidate over another (I have not yet heard the tape or seen a transcript so cannot remember exactly what was said).

'Sorry to ruin your holiday,' Moz said. 'But Ofcom have complained about this and we're having to look into it. It's quite serious. In fact I'm having a meeting about it later.'

'Are you calling me to tell me off then, Moz?' I asked. 'Are you calling to tell me not to do it again?'

He didn't really seem to know.

'This is just a shot in the dark,' I said. 'But are you sacking me?'

There was confused mumbling at the other end of the line.

'Are you suspending me?' I continued.

More confused mumbling.

'We're having a meeting to discuss it,' he finally said. 'I'll ring you later.'

I'd been sitting there without a worry, enjoying my meal and my holiday. This was like a blow to the stomach. Having discovered the reason for the call, I then went back inside to inform Melinda. The disbelief and hurt I saw in her eyes then still haunts me.

'If they haven't decided to sack you, then why are they even telling you? Why are they even hinting at it?' she exclaimed.

To be honest, after having life-threatening cancer, there isn't much that can hit you with the same kind of emotional wallop, but that conversation with Moz had worried and depressed me. If I was to lose my job it wasn't as if I had millions stashed away in some offshore account that we could live on for the rest of our lives. All the money we'd earned we'd spent!

We sat around that night waiting for the promised call but it never came. I rang Moz's mobile several times but it always went to voicemail. That night, nobody slept, not even the dogs. I managed to get hold of Moz two days later and I asked him what was happening. He wasn't very forthcoming. In fact, it seemed to me, he was trying to avoid giving me a straight answer.

'It looks really bad when it's written down,' he told me.

'Could you play the tape to me?' I asked him.

'Well, I haven't got it here,' he replied. 'But the transcript looks bad.'

'So are you fining me, suspending me, or what?' I continued.

'It's up to the board now,' he concluded.

'Fine. I'll be back on Sunday then.'

'No,' Moz told me. 'I think it would be better if you kept a low profile. Keep your head down for a few days. Let's wait until after the election. Don't come back to work until then.'

We then had a long discussion about whether I was being suspended or not. It all seemed so vague. All I wanted to know was when I could come back to work. I rang my agent, Stuart, and asked him what was going on, but he'd heard nothing either. The uncertainty was appalling.

So, for the next few days, we wandered around in a sort of mental fog. I had to tell my family we were having another week's 'holiday' as I'd been told not to say anything to anyone. Naturally, I was asked more than once if everything was alright.

From that Friday to the following Thursday we waited, not knowing what to do next. I have never felt so much in limbo. Stuart put in a call to Moz on the Thursday and was told that I could return to work unless I heard anything to the contrary.

The relief all around was enormous.

I was due to do a show for Meridian TV down in Southampton on the following day (Friday). I was driving down the M3 motorway when I got the phone call from Moz.

'I'm sorry, James,' he said. 'But the board have decided to terminate your contract with immediate effect.'

And that was it.

When you get that kind of information at any time it isn't good, but when you're driving down a motorway it can be positively hazardous. I pulled over to continue the conversation.

'So when do I get a chance to come and defend myself?' I enquired.

'The board have taken the decision,' he told me. 'Sorry, James.'

I was shocked. I'd never been given a warning. This momentous (well, momentous for me) decision came completely out of the blue.

I was also hurt. I had worked on talkSPORT and Talk Radio for thirteen years. That place was like my second home. I had always been under the impression that the people who ran that station liked and respected me. They might not always agree with me, but the world would be a pretty dull place if we all had the same opinions.

What hurt me even more was that no one was telling my audience. It was as if I'd just disappeared. Some listeners have since told me that they feared I had cancer again. Some of them have been with me on various radio stations for over twenty years. We're like a big family. We may be abusive to each other but we all take it in the spirit in which it's meant. And my listeners know that whatever I supposedly said to cause so much offence would have been said in my own style. I have no political leanings, despite some of the press insisting I'm a rabid right-winger.

So, in one fell swoop, talkSPORT had removed one of their main brands – because that is what my job had become, 'being James Whale'. With their help and promotion, that is what I'd achieved, and it was only with their backing and encouragement that I was able to broadcast the way I do.

As my listeners know, I like to put my point across and

some of those points are made fairly forcibly, but is that such a bad thing? My private belief with politics is that anyone who becomes a politician isn't actually fit to be one. Politicians should be there to represent the people, not their own parties and not their own individual needs. But that's just my own personal opinion, for what it's worth.

However, none of this helped as far as my predicament was concerned. In addition to terminating my contract, talkSPORT had also failed to offer any form of redundancy or severance package. I had gone, almost overnight, from earning pretty good money to earning virtually nothing. I'm not expecting sympathy, by the way, I'm merely stating the position I was in. I'd never been one to save for a rainy day. What I earned I spent. I redistributed my wealth the way Casanova distributed his seed. I spent money like it was going out of fashion. You tend to do this having had cancer.

So, Melinda and I were sitting around in our heavily mortgaged house wondering what the hell we were going to do, when my incredibly good friend Andy Hudson popped into my mind. Andy and his mate, Cris St Valery, run Bid TV, and they said they'd be happy for me to do a show for them. There are a number of satellite channels that offer a similar service but Bid TV is the best and I enjoy the shows I do for them. I also continue to review the newspapers on *Sky News*, usually on a Thursday, with my good friend Eamonn Holmes. The latest string to my bow, with a lot of encouragement and help from Keith Chegwin, is to set up my own radio station online. So www.jameswhaleradio.com is up and running. I have no idea how all this 'stuff' works but I was lucky, yet again, meeting someone called Kevin Millard, who is not only young, enthusiastic and on the same wavelength as me, but he also knows how it all works. So, every Tuesday evening with the help of www.playradiouk.com, I broadcast live, not only to Britain but to the whole world. I believe that the future of all broadcasting is online. Things will sort themselves out, I have no doubt of that, but I'd be lying if I said I didn't miss my show on talkSPORT. More than anything, of course, I miss my listeners. Hopefully they miss me too.

However, no one knows what the future holds and I feel sure that at some stage in months or years to come, I will be back where I belong. Dispensing wisdom, venom and abuse in equal measures. Pricking the pomposity of politicians and talentless wannabes everywhere. Either on TV, the radio or the Internet. Or even all three.

Keep your eyes and your ears open.

Above all, keep your options and opinions open.

They should have known better.